THE KIMMEL CENTER FOR THE PERFORMING ARTS

HOME OF THE PHILADELPHIA ORCHESTRA

Editor/Project Manager: David Updike

Art Director/Graphic Designer: Jennifer Urdang

Creative Director: Frank V. Pileggi

Director of Publications: Nancy L. Hebble

Director of Marketing and Communications: Sandra Horrocks

Acknowledgments:
Lynne Honickman, volunteer and Gala Preview Steering Committee
Matthew Singer, Contributing Editor
JoAnne E. Barry, Archivist, The Philadelphia Orchestra
Eric Sellen, Publications Manager, The Philadelphia Orchestra
Mary Louise Castaldi, Reference Librarian, The University of the Arts
Mark Germer, Music Librarian, The University of the Arts
Geraldine Duclow, Head, Theatre Collection, Free Library of Philadelphia
Jane Sanders, Photo Research Consultant

Printer: CRW Graphics

Bindery: Hoster Bindery, Inc.

The text and captions for this book were typeset in Giovanni, and the headings were typeset
in Engravers Gothic and Florentine Script. The book was printed on 100 lb. Garda Silk paper
and bound in Scholco Brillianta book cloth with 100 lb. Bravo Dull Offset end sheets.

THE KIMMEL CENTER FOR THE PERFORMING ARTS

HOME OF THE PHILADELPHIA ORCHESTRA

Text by Diana Burgwyn

Book design by Munroe Creative Partners

Philadelphia

Regional Performing Arts Center

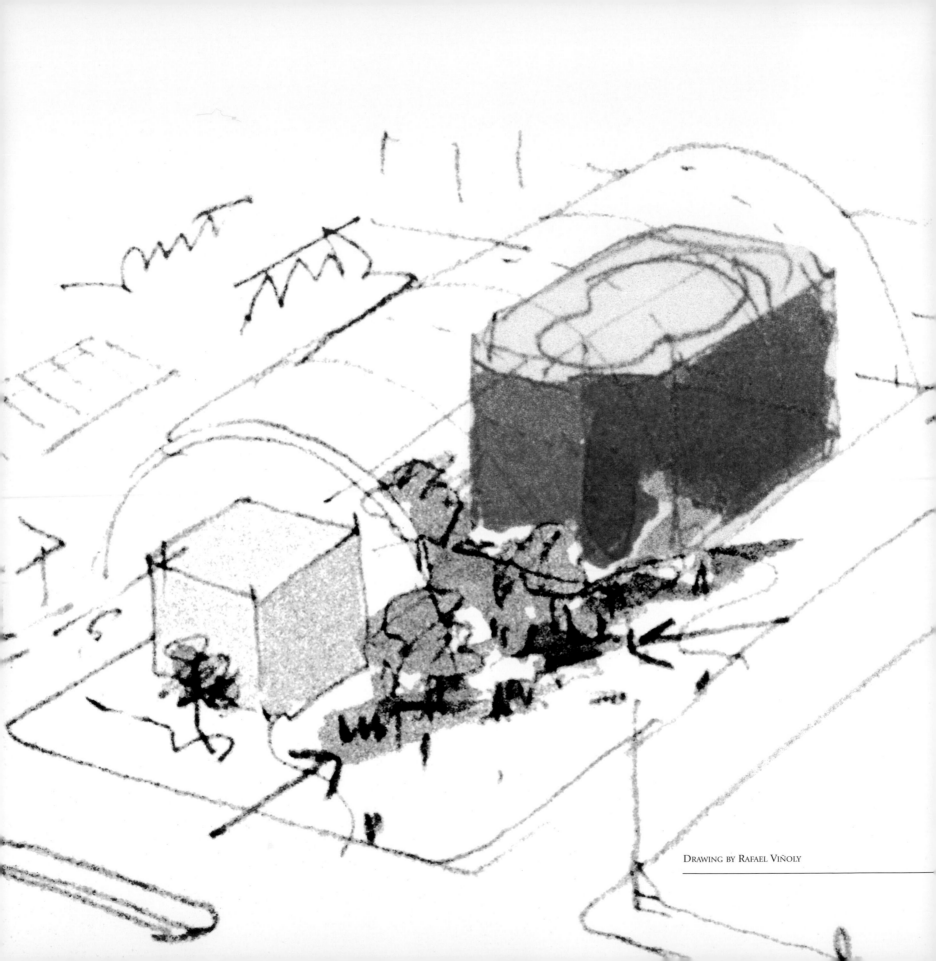

CONTENTS

A TRIBUTE TO SIDNEY KIMMEL

Are miracles a thing of the past? Not in Philadelphia. Glowing and magnificent, The Kimmel Center for the Performing Arts is proof that miracles happen—but only if a miracle-maker is at hand.

Sidney Kimmel's bold commitment to creating a world-class home for The Philadelphia Orchestra dates back to 1993 at a crucial time in the project's history. His historical gift and unprecedented support since then have been truly extraordinary. They have illuminated a way for all to join in building a landmark, a new symbol for Philadelphia, and cast the spotlight on a glorious future for the performing arts.

Sidney has spent much of his working life in the apparel industry, but that is only the starting point for his wide-ranging interests and philanthropic activities. His great business acumen is exceeded only by his special commitment to philanthropy, and that combination of professional skill and social conscience allows Sidney to touch the lives of so many. Established in 1993, The Sidney Kimmel Foundation has given in excess of $400 million, more than three-fourths of which has gone to advance health care and, in particular, cancer research. Sidney's recent gift to Johns Hopkins, which has renamed its comprehensive cancer center in his honor, underscores that today Sidney is recognized as one of the world's largest single donors to cancer research. Among many honors, he received the American Cancer Society's Humanitarian Award in 1999 and the American Jewish Committee's National Human Relations Award in 2000.

Sidney was raised just ten blocks from where The Kimmel Center now stands. How fitting it is, then, that this extraordinary building—which he did so much to shape—honors him. He has said, with characteristic grace and modesty, "I would never have imagined the good fortune of having my name associated with a hall of this stature." But we know that it is he who brought this dream to reality, and in doing so forever transformed the heart of his hometown, the great city of Philadelphia. We, like all Philadelphians, are enormously proud to count Sidney Kimmel as one of our own, and to applaud him.

Beyond his crucial role as benefactor, Sidney Kimmel has been a hands-on partner in this historic undertaking. The beauty of this state-of-the-art landmark that now graces the Avenue of the Arts bears the stamp of his equally keen business and aesthetic senses. A prescient champion of famed architect Rafael Viñoly—who in 1998 unveiled his breathtaking design for the Center—Sidney knew how to best nurture the design process as it evolved. It was especially gratifying to observe the warm and productive personal and professional relationship that grew between Sidney and Rafael, both of whom find inspiration in forms, shapes, finishes, and textures. The great architect says of his partner, "Sidney is a generous individual with a sense of aesthetics, a sense of civic pride, and a sense of history that are unique. While his level of financial success is certainly uncommon, Sidney has the 'common touch.' I'm a 'common' guy too, so we hit it off!"

To borrow a line from Shakespeare, The Kimmel Center "sits new-risen from a dream." In years to come, it will fill with the sights and sounds of performers who create the magic of art, and the audiences of all ages and interests who believe in that magic. We know that it is this lively and ever-changing mosaic of artists and audiences—of people and all their glorious possibilities—that inspired Sidney's vision. In the earliest days of this magnificent project, he described the performing arts center that would someday bear his name as "a gift to the future." Thanks to his generosity, the future is now! For that, for all he has brought to Philadelphia, and for his sharing with others, we express our gratitude and offer a warm thank you to Sidney Kimmel.

Willard G. Rouse III, Chair
Regional Performing Arts Center

Richard L. Smoot, Chair
The Philadelphia Orchestra Association

C. Christopher Cannon, Chair
Opera Company of Philadelphia

Louise H. Reed, Chair
Pennsylvania Ballet

Laurie Wagman, Founder/Chair
American Theater Arts for Youth

Kenneth M. Jarin, Co-Chair
Thomas J. Knox, Co-Chair
Chamber Orchestra of Philadelphia

Spencer Wertheimer, Chair
PHILADANCO

Jerry G. Rubenstein, Chair
Philadelphia Chamber Music Society

G. Fred DiBona, Jr., Chair
Peter Nero and the Philly Pops

ABOVE: SIDNEY KIMMEL

OPPOSITE PAGE: CAROLINE KIMMEL

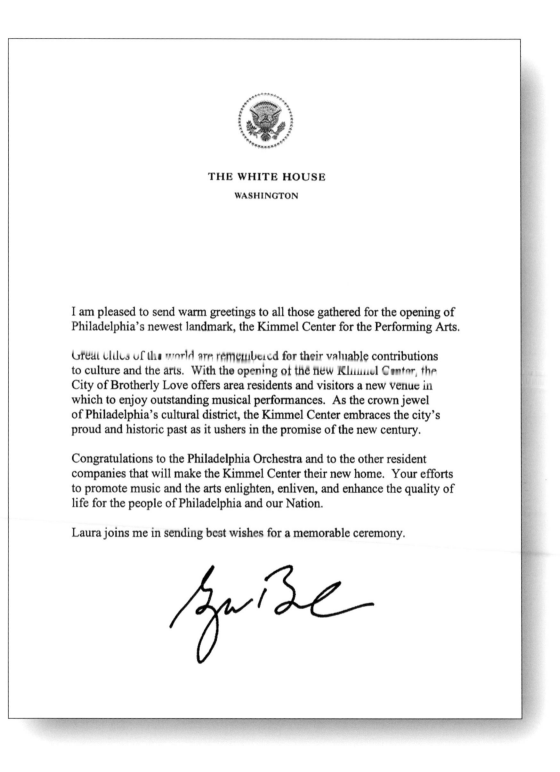

THE WHITE HOUSE

WASHINGTON

I am pleased to send warm greetings to all those gathered for the opening of Philadelphia's newest landmark, the Kimmel Center for the Performing Arts.

Great cities of the world are remembered for their valuable contributions to culture and the arts. With the opening of the new Kimmel Center, the City of Brotherly Love offers area residents and visitors a new venue in which to enjoy outstanding musical performances. As the crown jewel of Philadelphia's cultural district, the Kimmel Center embraces the city's proud and historic past as it ushers in the promise of the new century.

Congratulations to the Philadelphia Orchestra and to the other resident companies that will make the Kimmel Center their new home. Your efforts to promote music and the arts enlighten, enliven, and enhance the quality of life for the people of Philadelphia and our Nation.

Laura joins me in sending best wishes for a memorable ceremony.

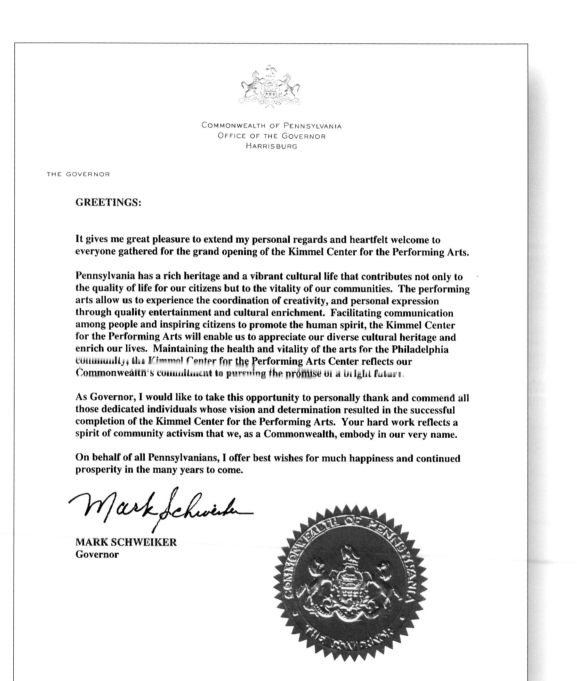

COMMONWEALTH OF PENNSYLVANIA
OFFICE OF THE GOVERNOR
HARRISBURG

THE GOVERNOR

GREETINGS:

It gives me great pleasure to extend my personal regards and heartfelt welcome to everyone gathered for the grand opening of the Kimmel Center for the Performing Arts.

Pennsylvania has a rich heritage and a vibrant cultural life that contributes not only to the quality of life for our citizens but to the vitality of our communities. The performing arts allow us to experience the coordination of creativity, and personal expression through quality entertainment and cultural enrichment. Facilitating communication among people and inspiring citizens to promote the human spirit, the Kimmel Center for the Performing Arts will enable us to appreciate our diverse cultural heritage and enrich our lives. Maintaining the health and vitality of the arts for the Philadelphia community, the Kimmel Center for the Performing Arts Center reflects our Commonwealth's commitment to pursuing the promise of a bright future.

As Governor, I would like to take this opportunity to personally thank and commend all those dedicated individuals whose vision and determination resulted in the successful completion of the Kimmel Center for the Performing Arts. Your hard work reflects a spirit of community activism that we, as a Commonwealth, embody in our very name.

On behalf of all Pennsylvanians, I offer best wishes for much happiness and continued prosperity in the many years to come.

MARK SCHWEIKER
Governor

United States Senate

WASHINGTON, DC 20510–3802

December 14, 2001

Dear Friends:

I am pleased to welcome you to the long-awaited opening of the Kimmel Center for the Performing Arts.

This magnificent structure will host visitors, concert-goers, and many of the greatest names in the performing arts from the city, the country, and the world. It will be the home of one of the world's greatest orchestras and of other extraordinarily talented groups from all over the region. The Kimmel Center, centerpiece of Philadelphia's fascinating and lively Avenue of the Arts, will also be a symbol of the excitement and promise of the city's dynamic growth.

Perhaps most importantly, the Kimmel Center will welcome and reach out to all the members of the Philadelphia community. I believe its beauty and accessibility will attract new friends of the arts.

Joan joins me in extending thanks to all those whose hard work and generosity has made the Kimmel Center possible and in sending our very best wishes for the Opening and the Inaugural Festival.

My best.

Sincerely,

Arlen Specter

December 14, 2001

Dear Friends:

It gives me great pleasure to welcome you to the Opening of the Kimmel Center for the Performing Arts.

Pennsylvanians have long recognized the important role the arts play in creating vital communities, spurring economic development, and attracting new workers and residents. The Kimmel Center will add another dimension to the Philadelphia region's stature as one of the nation's best places to live and work and will bolster its century-old reputation as a home of the arts.

The Kimmel Center also stands out as a true example of a public-private partnership. The far-sightedness of civic and governmental leaders and the generosity of the region's citizens combine to make the Kimmel Center a model for the arts development across the country.

I look forward to many opportunities to be part of the Kimmel Center audience, to participate in its educational activities, and to enjoy its beautiful space. I wish all of you a wonderful and stimulating inaugural weekend!

Sincerely,

Rick Santorum
United States Senate

Commonwealth of Pennsylvania

MARK S. SCHWEIKER, GOVERNOR
ROBERT C. JUBELIRER, LIEUTENANT GOVERNOR

SENATE

MARK R. CORRIGAN, SECRETARY PARLIAMENTARIAN

W. RUSSELL FABER, CHIEF CLERK

MAJORITY OFFICERS

DAVID J. BRIGHTBILL, MAJORITY FLOOR LEADER

JEFFREY E. PICCOLA, MAJORITY WHIP

NOAH W. WENGER, MAJORITY CAUCUS CHAIR

ROBERT D. ROBBINS, MAJORITY CAUCUS SECRETARY

ROBERT J. THOMPSON, MAJORITY APPROPRIATIONS
COMMITTEE CHAIR

JOE CONTI, MAJORITY POLICY COMMITTEE CHAIR

MARY JO WHITE, MAJORITY CAUCUS ADMINISTRATOR

MINORITY OFFICERS

ROBERT J. MELLOW, MINORITY FLOOR LEADER

MICHAEL A. O'PAKE, MINORITY WHIP

JACK WAGNER, MINORITY CAUCUS CHAIR

RAPHAEL J. MUSTO, MINORITY CAUCUS SECRETARY

VINCENT J. FUMO, MINORITY APPROPRIATIONS COMMITTEE CHAIR

RICHARD A. KASUNIC, MINORITY POLICY COMMITTEE CHAIR

J. BARRY STOUT, MINORITY CAUCUS ADMINISTRATOR

HOUSE OF REPRESENTATIVES

MAJORITY LEADERSHIP

MATTHEW J. RYAN, SPEAKER

JOHN M. PERZEL, MAJORITY LEADER

SAMUEL H. SMITH, MAJORITY WHIP

DAVID G. ARGALL, MAJORITY CAUCUS CHAIR

ELINOR Z. TAYLOR, MAJORITY CAUCUS SECRETARY

ROY W. CORNELL, MAJORITY POLICY CHAIR

MERLE H. PHILLIPS, MAJORITY CAUCUS ADMINISTRATOR

JOHN E. BARLEY, MAJORITY APPROPRIATIONS CHAIR

MINORITY LEADERSHIP

H. WILLIAM DEWEESE, DEMOCRATIC LEADER

MICHAEL R. VEON, DEMOCRATIC WHIP

MARK B. COHEN, DEMOCRATIC CAUCUS CHAIR

JEFFREY W. COY, DEMOCRATIC CAUCUS SECRETARY

VICTOR J. LESCOVITZ, DEMOCRATIC POLICY CHAIR

FRED BELARDI, DEMOCRATIC CAUCUS ADMINISTRATOR

DWIGHT EVANS, DEMOCRATIC APPROPRIATIONS CHAIR

City of Philadelphia

JOHN F. STREET, MAYOR

CITY COUNCIL

ANNA C. VERNA, PRESIDENT

MARIE B. HAUSER, CHIEF CLERK

COUNCILMEMBERS-AT-LARGE

BLONDELL REYNOLDS BROWN (D)

DAVID COHEN (D)

W. WILSON GOODE, JR. (D)

JAMES F. KENNEY (D)

W. THACHER LONGSTRETH (R)

ANGEL ORTIZ (D)

FRANK RIZZO (R)

DISTRICT COUNCIL MEMBERS

JANNIE L. BLACKWELL (D) – DISTRICT 3

DARRELL L. CLARKE (D) – DISTRICT 5

FRANK DiCICCO (D) – DISTRICT 1

JOAN L. KRAJEWSKI (D) – DISTRICT 6

RICHARD T. MARIANO (D) – DISTRICT 7

DONNA REED MILLER (D) – DISTRICT 8

MICHAEL A. NUTTER (D) – DISTRICT 4

BRIAN J. O'NEILL (R)- DISTRICT 10

MARIAN B. TASCO (D) – DISTRICT 9

ANNA C. VERNA (D) – DISTRICT 2

CITY OF PHILADELPHIA

OFFICE OF THE MAYOR
ROOM 215 CITY HALL
PHILADELPHIA, PENNSYLVANIA 19107-3295
(215) 686-2181
FAX (215) 686-2180

JOHN F. STREET
MAYOR

December 14, 2001

Greetings:

This is a proud and exciting day for every resident of the Philadelphia region. A dazzling landmark has risen on the Avenue of the Arts – The Kimmel Center for the Performing Arts. It is spectacular evidence of the City of Philadelphia's spirit and vitality and an unparalleled gathering place and arts center for Philadelphians and visitors from around the world.

The Kimmel Center takes to an even higher stage this great city's preeminent role as a showcase for the performing arts. Home to an impressive roster of resident companies – including one of our nation's greatest cultural ambassadors, The Philadelphia Orchestra – The Kimmel Center will also host touring companies and productions that will bring the greatest names in the arts and the broadest range of audiences to the Avenue of the Arts.

My friend and predecessor in the Mayor's Office, Ed Rendell, envisioned the Avenue of the Arts as a "crème-de-la-crème, European-style arts district," and referred to The Kimmel Center as "the most important project in Philadelphia." Today, with The Kimmel Center as its anchor, the Avenue of the Arts fulfills this vision of a great cultural crossroads, one that celebrates the region's rich artistic heritage, and welcomes a new century's greatest performers.

I congratulate Chairman Willard G. Rouse III, President Leslie Anne Miller, and all those whose leadership and untiring efforts have made this important dream a reality. We extend our sincerest thanks to Sidney Kimmel for leading the way in making this one of the finest and most beautiful performing arts centers in the nation. Fired by Rafael Viñoly's breathtaking design, and his own profound sense of civic commitment, Sidney Kimmel set a spark illuminating the great promise the Center held for our hometown and the entire region. We applaud him for recognizing – and reminding the rest of us – that Philadelphia deserves the very best.

With kind regard, I am

John F. Street, Esq.
Mayor

With great pleasure, I welcome you to The Kimmel Center for the Performing Arts.

I have helped to create many other buildings over the years, but this one is something special. In its beauty and vitality it stands for a resurgent city. And in a time of hesitancy and fear, its arching glass dome reminds us that, now and ever, the performing arts are about hope, and are part of the strength and spirit of our community.

We, therefore, commit ourselves to a Kimmel Center that welcomes every segment of a widely diverse population. It will be people-friendly, arts-friendly, and technology-friendly—a reminder that the arts belong to all of us. A promise of cultural democracy.

This building—a partnership of the performing arts, architecture, and civic energy—represents a gift of service from many in our community to everyone in our community. While mentioning names always leaves someone out, the following individuals, families, corporations, and foundations deserve special recognition—for those who are not mentioned, of which there are hundreds, we hope you will understand: Sidney Kimmel, Ruth and Ray Perelman, the late Bob Casey, Tom Ridge, Midge and Ed Rendell, John Street, Verizon, Merck, The Annenberg Foundation, The Independence Foundation, The William Penn Foundation, The Pew Charitable Trusts, Peter Benoliel, Nora Brownell, Ted Burtis, the Haas family, Dodo Hamilton, Gerry and Marguerite Lenfest, Sam McCullough, Leslie Anne Miller, Stephanie Naidoff, Joe Neubauer, Dick Smoot, Manny Stamatakis, and the Board of Directors and staff of the Regional Performing Arts Center.

Unprecedented leadership spurred by the idea of The Kimmel Center reflects your determination that Philadelphia deserves the best. Whether The Kimmel Center is the world-class accomplishment we dreamed of will be judged by generations to come. What is already clear is that the response of this community has most certainly been world class. And the return on that investment will come in the faces of thousands of children, over many years. More than a legacy, more than a landmark, The Kimmel Center is a lasting tribute to your belief in Philadelphia.

And so, on behalf of all of us who have had the opportunity to serve as part of this magnificent undertaking, let me thank you again, and wish all of you the blessings of the holiday season and of peace.

Willard G. Rouse III, Chair

Welcome to the Inaugural Festivities of The Kimmel Center for the Performing Arts. This weekend we open the doors of The Kimmel Center, and with them a doorway to the arts in a city whose name has long been synonymous with the arts.

Inaugural events are traditional times to speak of renewal and change, and to offer thanks. And we have much for which to be thankful. As Philadelphians, we have been given a splendid heritage. Today, as is the duty of every generation, we add to that heritage, promising to honor and preserve what is best from the past, and to enlarge upon it for the benefit of our children.

In that spirit, we open the doors of this iconic piece of architecture, this great civic space, uniquely designed and set in a 21st-century urban context. We also lay the foundation for a great institution, which we pledge to administer with the common sense and passionate commitment of the ancient ideal that has long placed the arts at the center of every great civilization.

And in relying on the common energies, wisdom, and generosity of our community, we enlarge the boundaries of the possible. We already see The Kimmel Center's economic impact and the increased appeal of Philadelphia as a place to visit, live, and enjoy a rich diversity. As The Kimmel Center encourages traditional arts audiences to sample new kinds of performances, educates learners of all ages to become new audiences, and entices visitors from across the country and the world, we demonstrate again that, galvanized by a vision, there is nothing Philadelphia cannot do.

In all these ways, The Kimmel Center is truly a community project—reflecting, serving, and welcoming all our citizens in its grand public plaza, arts education center, and gathering places, small and large. Our doors will be open every day. Our venues will be home to The Philadelphia Orchestra and seven other Resident Companies. To their enormous talents we add a great array of dance, theatrical, and musical performances, guided by our commitment to serve the broadest possible spectrum of the community.

The Kimmel Center represents the brains of its great design team, and the spirit of its courageous construction crew, but its heart comes from you. Your generosity and your unflagging support have brought it to life. Generations of audiences will watch the special magic of the performing arts in this special space, and on behalf of them we offer our gratitude and thanks.

The present world situation is without parallel, and our own country faces unprecedented challenges. They have brought forth the national virtues of courage and patriotism. The extraordinary performers who come to our beautiful halls will offer the comforting virtues of solace and inspiration.

Today, all eyes are on Philadelphia—and we have never looked better. Our beautiful and welcoming city has made another bold beginning. And in this place may our days be full of beauty and joy, as we greet the future with confidence.

Leslie Anne Miller, President

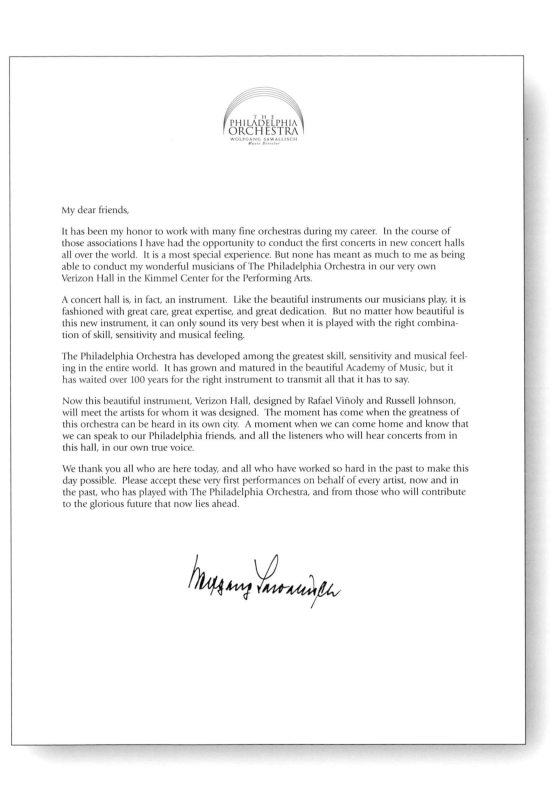

My dear friends,

It has been my honor to work with many fine orchestras during my career. In the course of those associations I have had the opportunity to conduct the first concerts in new concert halls all over the world. It is a most special experience. But none has meant as much to me as being able to conduct my wonderful musicians of The Philadelphia Orchestra in our very own Verizon Hall in the Kimmel Center for the Performing Arts.

A concert hall is, in fact, an instrument. Like the beautiful instruments our musicians play, it is fashioned with great care, great expertise, and great dedication. But no matter how beautiful is this new instrument, it can only sound its very best when it is played with the right combination of skill, sensitivity and musical feeling.

The Philadelphia Orchestra has developed among the greatest skill, sensitivity and musical feeling in the entire world. It has grown and matured in the beautiful Academy of Music, but it has waited over 100 years for the right instrument to transmit all that it has to say.

Now this beautiful instrument, Verizon Hall, designed by Rafael Viñoly and Russell Johnson, will meet the artists for whom it was designed. The moment has come when the greatness of this orchestra can be heard in its own city. A moment when we can come home and know that we can speak to our Philadelphia friends, and all the listeners who will hear concerts from in this hall, in our own true voice.

We thank you all who are here today, and all who have worked so hard in the past to make this day possible. Please accept these very first performances on behalf of every artist, now and in the past, who has played with The Philadelphia Orchestra, and from those who will contribute to the glorious future that now lies ahead.

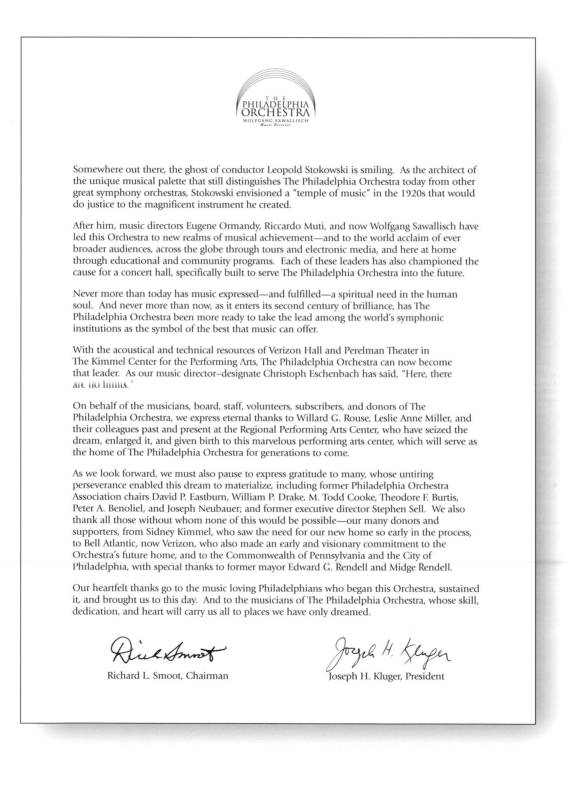

Somewhere out there, the ghost of conductor Leopold Stokowski is smiling. As the architect of the unique musical palette that still distinguishes The Philadelphia Orchestra today from other great symphony orchestras, Stokowski envisioned a "temple of music" in the 1920s that would do justice to the magnificent instrument he created.

After him, music directors Eugene Ormandy, Riccardo Muti, and now Wolfgang Sawallisch have led this Orchestra to new realms of musical achievement—and to the world acclaim of ever broader audiences, across the globe through tours and electronic media, and here at home through educational and community programs. Each of these leaders has also championed the cause for a concert hall, specifically built to serve The Philadelphia Orchestra into the future.

Never more than today has music expressed—and fulfilled—a spiritual need in the human soul. And never more than now, as it enters its second century of brilliance, has The Philadelphia Orchestra been more ready to take the lead among the world's symphonic institutions as the symbol of the best that music can offer.

With the acoustical and technical resources of Verizon Hall and Perelman Theater in The Kimmel Center for the Performing Arts, The Philadelphia Orchestra can now become that leader. As our music director–designate Christoph Eschenbach has said, "Here, there are no limits."

On behalf of the musicians, board, staff, volunteers, subscribers, and donors of The Philadelphia Orchestra, we express eternal thanks to Willard G. Rouse, Leslie Anne Miller, and their colleagues past and present at the Regional Performing Arts Center, who have seized the dream, enlarged it, and given birth to this marvelous performing arts center, which will serve as the home of The Philadelphia Orchestra for generations to come.

As we look forward, we must also pause to express gratitude to many, whose untiring perseverance enabled this dream to materialize, including former Philadelphia Orchestra Association chairs David P. Eastburn, William P. Drake, M. Todd Cooke, Theodore F. Burtis, Peter A. Benoliel, and Joseph Neubauer; and former executive director Stephen Sell. We also thank all those without whom none of this would be possible—our many donors and supporters, from Sidney Kimmel, who saw the need for our new home so early in the process, to Bell Atlantic, now Verizon, who also made an early and visionary commitment to the Orchestra's future home, and to the Commonwealth of Pennsylvania and the City of Philadelphia, with special thanks to former mayor Edward G. Rendell and Midge Rendell.

Our heartfelt thanks go to the music loving Philadelphians who began this Orchestra, sustained it, and brought us to this day. And to the musicians of The Philadelphia Orchestra, whose skill, dedication, and heart will carry us all to places we have only dreamed.

Richard L. Smoot, Chairman

Joseph H. Kluger, President

KIMMEL CENTER OPENING CELEBRATION

*D*ecember 16–31, 2001, a star-studded, imaginative, and diverse spectrum of programs will welcome and delight The Kimmel Center's first-ever audiences. The Opening Celebration, presented by Lincoln Financial Group, showcases the unending possibilities of The Kimmel Center with amazing performances in Verizon Hall and Perelman Theater and free programming throughout The Kimmel Center's many public venues. In addition, benefit events and special holiday performances by Resident Companies bring the best in music and dance to Verizon Hall, Perelman Theater, and the Academy of Music.

GRAND OPENING

SUNDAY, DECEMBER 16, 2001

The Kimmel Center opens at 11 A.M. with a ribbon-cutting ceremony. From 11 A.M. to 4 P.M., enjoy *The Kimmel Center Performs—An Artistic Open House*, featuring free live entertainment, artistic interactive activities, and workshops in jazz, dance, costume design, theater, storytelling, and poetry.

ONGOING

THROUGH DECEMBER 31, 2001

DAILY: Free Tours of The Kimmel Center and the Academy of Music | NOON–1:30 P.M.: Free Lunchtime Concerts in Commonwealth Plaza | 5–8 P.M.: Happy Hours in Commonwealth Plaza with free live performances | **Plus**: Post-concert jam sessions, dancing, caroling, and cabaret in Commonwealth Plaza, and weekend family programming

KYW-3 AND PENNSYLVANIA BALLET PRESENT GEORGE BALANCHINE'S *THE NUTCRACKER*

DECEMBER 14–31
ACADEMY OF MUSIC

A performance like no other, Pennsylvania Ballet's *The Nutcracker* features all the splendor Philadelphia audiences expect! More than a beautiful ballet, more than a momentous cultural event, *The Nutcracker* has become an extraordinary tradition shared by families and friends of every generation.

AN INAUGURAL PERFORMANCE BY THE CHAMBER ORCHESTRA OF PHILADELPHIA

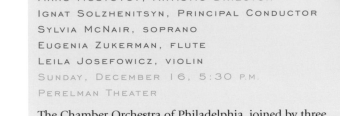

MARC MOSTOVOY, ARTISTIC DIRECTOR
IGNAT SOLZHENITSYN, PRINCIPAL CONDUCTOR
SYLVIA MCNAIR, SOPRANO
EUGENIA ZUKERMAN, FLUTE
LEILA JOSEFOWICZ, VIOLIN
SUNDAY, DECEMBER 16, 5:30 P.M.
PERELMAN THEATER

The Chamber Orchestra of Philadelphia, joined by three internationally renowned American musicians, formally opens Perelman Theater with a magnificent concert and gala dinner. Marc Mostovoy will conduct and Ignat Solzhenitsyn will both solo at the piano and conduct in this memorable concert, which includes Beethoven's *Consecration of the House Overture*, as well as popular selections by Mozart, Canteloube, and Sarasate, and a specially commissioned world premiere dedicatory fanfare.

HOLIDAY POPS! WITH PETER NERO AND THE PHILLY POPS®

PRESENTED BY ENCORE SERIES, INC.
MONDAY, DECEMBER 17, 8 P.M.
TUESDAY, DECEMBER 18, 8 P.M.
VERIZON HALL

Now in its 23rd season, the POPS is one of the most versatile performing groups in the country. Its blend of jazz, light classics, music from Broadway and Hollywood, plus excerpts from the symphonic repertoire, is played by a talented group of instrumentalists from the Philadelphia area.

A Resident Company at The Kimmel Center, the POPS has been led from the beginning by Grammy Award–winner Peter Nero, a conductor, virtuoso pianist, composer, and arranger with more than 60 albums to his credit.

AUDRA MCDONALD

PHILADELPHIA SOLO DEBUT
WEDNESDAY, DECEMBER 19, 8 P.M.
VERIZON HALL

Three-time Tony Award-winning singer Audra McDonald has been acclaimed the future of serious music theater. Trained at Juilliard, the sensuous-voiced soprano started her Broadway climb with the celebrated 1993 revival of *Carousel*, for which she earned her first Tony. Another Tony was awarded for her role as an aspiring opera singer in Terrence McNally's hit drama *Master Class*, and a third for her leading role in the musical *Ragtime*. McDonald's 1998 solo debut album, *Way Back to Paradise*, was named Adult Record of the Year by the *New York Times*. She endeared herself to television audiences in ABC's *Annie*, appeared in Mike Nichols's television movie *Wit*, and has been a guest with major orchestras, including The New York Philharmonic and The Philadelphia Orchestra. Entire shows have been created to showcase her talents, including LaChiusa's 1999 *Marie Christine*.

OPENING NIGHT BENEFIT
THE PHILADELPHIA CHAMBER
MUSIC SOCIETY

WEDNESDAY, DECEMBER 19, 8 P.M.
PERELMAN THEATER

The Philadelphia Chamber Music Society, founded in 1985 and now a Resident Company of The Kimmel Center, is one of the world's foremost presenters of chamber music and recitals by internationally acclaimed artists, with an annual program of more than 50 performances and nearly 40 educational programs. This Opening Night Benefit will feature special performances by the Guarneri and Tokyo String Quartets, followed by a champagne and dessert reception.

BRANFORD MARSALIS QUARTET
JOSHUA REDMAN QUARTET

THURSDAY, DECEMBER 20, 8 P.M.
VERIZON HALL

Branford Marsalis (whose father, Ellis, and younger brothers, Wynton and Delfeayo, are also esteemed jazz musicians) formed his quartet in 1987 after stints with Art Blakey, Herbie Hancock, Clark Terry, brother Wynton's quintet, and Sting. From 1992 to 1998, he also led the house band of the *Tonight Show*.

Marsalis's many recordings, which feature him on alto, tenor, and soprano saxophone, include *Buckshot La Fonque*, *Crazy People Music*, *Requiem*, and *Contemporary Jazz*, which won a Grammy for Best Jazz Instrumental Album. His classical credentials are impeccable as well. His 2001 release, *Creation*, is a collaboration with the Orpheus Chamber Orchestra, and features the works of Debussy, Fauré, Ibert, Milhaud, Ravel, and Satie.

———

Joshua Redman, son of legendary tenor saxophonist Dewey Redman, studied recorder, guitar, and piano before turning to his father's instrument. Redman graduated summa cum laude from Harvard. Accepted at Yale University Law School, Redman instead moved to Brooklyn, where he began playing the sax regularly.

In 1991, he won the Thelonious Monk International Jazz Saxophone Competition, earning a recording contract with Warner Brothers. One award followed another: the *Jazz Times* Reader's Poll voted him Best New Artist for 1992; in 1993, *Rolling Stone* named him Hot Jazz Artist, and the *Down Beat* critics' poll called him the No. 1 Tenor Saxophonist Deserving of Wider Recognition.

Since his 1993 eponymous debut with Warner Brothers, Redman has recorded *Wish*, *Freedom in the Groove*, *Timeless Tales*, and *Beyond*. On his latest recording, *Passage of Time*, his most ambitious to date, he was both composer and bandleader. Redman was artistic director and artist-in-residence for the 2000 San Francisco Jazz Festival.

VIENNA CHOIR BOYS

WITH ASSISTING HARPIST
ELIZABETH HAINEN DEPETERS
FRIDAY, DECEMBER 21, 8 P.M.
VERIZON HALL

Audiences have thrilled for five centuries to the pure tones of the Vienna Choir Boys, whose origins can be found in a 1498 decree of Maximilian I that added six boys to the musicians of the imperial court. In later years, the ranks of the Court Choir Boys included not only promising young voices but several destined to be great composers—Joseph Haydn, Franz Schubert, and Anton Bruckner, among them. With the 1918 demise of the Austro-Hungarian Empire, the name was changed to Vienna Choir Boys.

Since that time, the ensemble has become known as Austria's "singing ambassadors." The Choir Boys' repertoire is a mix of classical, international folk songs, and waltzes and polkas by Johann Strauss. Among their selections will be Benjamin Britten's beloved *Ceremony of Carols,* composed in 1942 and consisting of ten carols based on anonymous medieval texts. Its haunting quality is enhanced by harp accompaniment, played by Elizabeth Hainen DePeters, Principal Harp of The Philadelphia Orchestra.

KLEZMER CONSERVATORY BAND

SATURDAY, DECEMBER 22, 8 P.M.
VERIZON HALL

Klezmer music, which originated in the folk, dance, and religious tunes played by itinerant Jewish musicians of medieval times, is enjoying a revival, with the Klezmer Conservatory Band in the forefront.

A 21-year-old ensemble begun by composer, instrumentalist, and conservatory instructor Hankus Netsky, the Klezmer Conservatory Band inspires audiences to cheers and tears. These fine musicians have mastered the myriad influences—Greek, Slavic, Turkish, Romany, and jazz—that have interwoven with klezmer's Jewish roots. The group was featured in the 1988 documentary film *A Jumpin' Night in the Garden of Eden*, and in the film *Enemies: A Love Story*. The ensemble won enthusiastic new fans though the PBS television special, "In the Fiddler's House," a collaboration with violinist Itzhak Perlman, which later was made into a recording. Featured musicians include vocalist Judy Bressler and clarinetist Irene Stahl.

CANADIAN BRASS

WITH THE PHILADELPHIA BRASS ENSEMBLE

SUNDAY, DECEMBER 23, 2 P.M.
VERIZON HALL

The five virtuosi of the Canadian Brass form an instantly recognizable ensemble, their unique sound combining brilliance with pinpoint precision in a repertoire that goes from baroque to contemporary.

Springing from a modest experiment in Toronto in 1970, the "fabulous five" revived the brass quintet's prominence. With a base of orchestral and chamber music, they developed a special affinity for the compositions of Johann Sebastian Bach. They then tackled later

composers, including Beethoven and Wagner, and took daring leaps into jazz, contemporary concert music, and pop songs. Some of their appearances are formal classical concerts, while others pair music with lively dialogue and theatrical effects. Their unique interpretation of Duke Ellington's "Take the A Train" received a 2000 Grammy nomination in the crossover category.

The Canadian Brass will be joined in works for double brass choir by the Philadelphia Brass Ensemble (all members of The Philadelphia Orchestra): David Bilger and Jeffrey Curnow (trumpet), Adam Unsworth (horn), Nitzan Haroz (trombone), and Blair Bollinger (bass trombone).

FIESTA LATINO WITH JIMMY BOSCH

WEDNESDAY, DECEMBER 26, 8 P.M.
VERIZON HALL

Drawing on an eclectic repertoire, Jimmy Bosch fuses the plenas of rural Puerto Rico, the Afro-Cuban mambo, the Beatles, American folk tunes, and the New York *salsa dura* (hard salsa) of the 1970s with straight-ahead jazz and contemporary rock. Thanks to Bosch, the progressive sound, complex rhythms, and socially conscious lyrics of *salsa dura* have earned new fans nationwide.

Born in Hoboken, New Jersey, Bosch frequented clubs in New York City, trombone in hand, playing as a sideman with many of the greats of Latin music. In 1978, while a student at Rutgers University, Bosch was hired by Andy Gonzalez to work with Conjunto Libre, initiating a prolific career and extensive discography that now spans two decades (including the Grammy-nominated *Caravana Cubana*). More recently, he moved to the front of the bandstand as leader of his own group, featuring some of the best singers and instrumentalists in the business.

MICHAEL FEINSTEIN

BETTY BUCKLEY

ON BROADWAY

THURSDAY, DECEMBER 27, 8 P.M.
VERIZON HALL

Michael Feinstein's warm voice, suave piano, and ebullient stage presence accompany his dedication to the songwriter's craft. He began his career as Ira Gershwin's assistant and soon developed a knack for bringing lost lyrics and forgotten orchestrations back to light. His extensive discography began with the 1985 *Pure Gershwin* and continued with the music of such luminaries as Irving Berlin, Jerome Kern, Jerry Herman, Cole Porter, and Jule Styne. Feinstein has recorded his own compositions as well, including "For Love Alone," on the album *Such Sweet Sorrow*. On his 2000 double-CD release, *Romance on Film/Romance on Broadway*, Feinstein delivers heartfelt interpretations of the great romantic ballads from films and Broadway musicals.

Feinstein first entered the performance spotlight in 1986 with appearances at the Algonquin Hotel and Carnegie Hall. He then moved to Broadway, where he triumphed in a one-man show. He appeared in and scored original music for *Get Bruce* and did a number of PBS specials, including "Michael Feinstein and Friends." In 1999, he saw a longtime dream come true with the opening of Feinstein's at The Regency, an elegant and intimate showcase for the greatest singers and cabaret performers.

———

Betty Buckley is a true Broadway diva. She won a Tony Award as Grizzabella in *Cats* (introducing American audiences to the song "Memory"), played the larger-than-life Norma Desmond in *Sunset Boulevard*, and created the role of Miss Alice Nutting, the music hall "male impersonator" in the musical version of the unfinished Dickens novel, *The Mystery of Edwin Drood*.

Buckley has been described as "a singer whose instrument is a peerless melding of vulnerability and power" (*Variety*). Her concerts with longtime piano accompanist Kenny Werner mix famous show tunes, country & western, and contemporary pop.

As an actress, she has appeared in a number of feature films, including *Tender Mercies* and Woody Allen's *Another Woman*, and on television in a variety of parts, including her starring role in the popular series *Eight Is Enough*. She is also a regular on *Oz*, the highly popular HBO prison drama.

Buckley's latest CD release is *Heart to Heart*. Among other albums is a live recording of her spectacular Carnegie Hall concert in 1996, a benefit for Broadway Cares/Equity Fights AIDS.

ST. PETERSBURG STATE BALLET ON ICE

SLEEPING BEAUTY ON ICE
SATURDAY, DECEMBER 29, 2 P.M.
SATURDAY, DECEMBER 29, 8 P.M.
SUNDAY, DECEMBER 30, 2 P.M.
VERIZON HALL

Russia and ballet: the two are inextricably linked. In 1967, ice was added to the mix. The remarkable St. Petersburg State Ballet on Ice, with 35 champion dancers/skaters, gained worldwide fame for its technical prowess and sensitive artistry. With elaborate costumes, full opera-house sets, and exquisite choreography, the company brings some of the most beloved full-length works of the ballet into a new realm.

Tchaikovsky's musical rendering of *Sleeping Beauty*, the story of a princess who is sent into a deep sleep from which she can only be awakened by the kiss of true love, has been an audience favorite for generations.

Under the leadership of General Director Mikhail Kaminov, a champion figure skater in Russia, and Principal Choreographer Konstantin Rassadin, a former principal dancer and choreographer for the fabled Kirov Ballet, the company has completed four highly successful North American tours since 1995.

Creating ice rinks out of concert halls requires 6,500 pounds of ice and a full day's labor in advance of the first performance.

NEW YEAR'S EVE CONCERT
THE PHILADELPHIA ORCHESTRA

WOLFGANG SAWALLISCH, CONDUCTOR
GABRIELE FONTANA, SOPRANO
MONDAY, DECEMBER 31, 8 P.M.
VERIZON HALL

The Orchestra's annual New Year's Eve Concert features traditional Viennese favorites—including tuneful waltzes, lively polkas, and operatic gems—to welcome in a new calendar year and toast the Orchestra's new home at The Kimmel Center.

GALA PREVIEW, DECEMBER 14 15, 2001

THE KIMMEL CENTER FOR THE PERFORMING ARTS

Friday Evening, December 14, 2001, 7:00 P.M. • Gala Preview Concert

VERIZON HALL • THE KIMMEL CENTER INAUGURAL GALA

MEMBERS OF THE PHILADELPHIA ORCHESTRA
WOLFGANG SAWALLISCH, CONDUCTOR
COPLAND, *FANFARE FOR THE COMMON MAN*

HORNS:
NOLAN MILLER
DAVID WETHERILL
DANIEL WILLIAMS
JEFFRY KIRSCHEN
ADAM UNSWORTH
SHELLEY SHOWERS

TRUMPETS:
DAVID BILGER
JEFFREY CURNOW
ROBERT W. EARLEY
ROGER BLACKBURN

TROMBONES:
NITZAN HAROZ
MATTHEW VAUGHN
ERIC CARLSON
BLAIR BOLLINGER

TUBA:
PAUL KRZYWICKI

TIMPANI:
DON S. LIUZZI

PERCUSSION:
MICHAEL BOOKSPAN
ANTHONY ORLANDO
ANGELA ZATOR NELSON

ANDRÉ WATTS, PIANO
BERNSTEIN, OVERTURE TO *CANDIDE*
TRANSCRIBED FOR PIANO BY ANDRÉ WATTS

DENYCE GRAVES, MEZZO-SOPRANO
FREDERICA VON STADE, MEZZO-SOPRANO
WARREN JONES, PIANO
PROGRAM TO BE ANNOUNCED

SIR ELTON JOHN

ABOUT THE COMPOSERS

AARON COPLAND
b. November 14, 1900
d. December 2, 1990

Brooklyn-born Aaron Copland was, in his own words, "preoccupied with writing serious concert music that would have a specifically American flavor." This is precisely what he accomplished, becoming the first composer whose music was considered outside the United States to be distinctly American.

Copland's earliest works were heavily influenced by jazz rhythms, but he soon shifted to a more austere and abstract style. In the mid-1930s, hoping to make his music more accessible to the general public, he began moving toward simplicity and melody. The music he created during this, his most productive period, has become a cornerstone of the concert world. Many of these works incorporate strong elements of American folk music, notably in the ballets *Billy the Kid*, *Rodeo*, and *Appalachian Spring*. Copland also composed a good deal of film music at this time, as well as the narrated *Lincoln Portrait* and *El salón México*, an orchestral piece based on Mexican folk music.

Composed in 1942, *Fanfare for the Common Man* premiered the following year with the Cincinnati Symphony Orchestra. Scored for brass and percussion, the work was commissioned by Cincinnati as a tribute to soldiers serving in World War II. In all, 18 composers contributed fanfares to this project, but Copland's is the only one that entered the standard repertoire.

The urgent pounding of kettledrums opens *Fanfare*, which continues with a simple brass theme in unison that is later harmonized in Copland's typically spare but grand fashion. Sentimental and somber, yet somehow reassuring, the work takes a mere three-and-one-half minutes to play. It has become one of the most recognizable themes in classical music.

LEONARD BERNSTEIN
b. August 25, 1918
d. October 14, 1990

Leonard Bernstein is one of the most remarkable figures in 20th-century music. He was catapulted into fame in 1943, at age 25, when, as assistant conductor of the New York Philharmonic, he substituted at the last minute for ailing conductor Bruno Walter. From that day, he retained a hold on the public imagination that, if anything, is stronger today, more than a decade after his death.

Bernstein was the complete musician, not only as a conductor but also as an educator who, through his television appearances and writings, made classical music understandable and appealing to both children and adults. A composer of astonishing breadth, he contributed to the symphonic, operatic, and choral repertoire, as well as Broadway, notably the beloved *West Side Story*.

Candide, which now has an equally devoted, if smaller, audience, is based on the Voltaire novel of that name, which satirized the fashionable philosophies of the 18th century. As adapted by Lillian Hellman and Richard Wilbur, it received mixed reviews upon its 1956 opening in New York. The show went through several revisions, finally achieving critical and popular success in 1973.

The ebullient overture to *Candide*, being performed in a unique piano version by André Watts, is written in the sonata allegro form, common to classical music but highly unusual for Broadway shows. Two contrasting vocal numbers from the work make their first appearance here in instrumental form: "Oh Happy We" and, as the coda, "Glitter and Be Gay."

ABOUT THE ARTISTS

ANDRÉ WATTS

Pianist André Watts was just shy of 10 years old when he first performed with The Philadelphia Orchestra, playing a Haydn concerto at a Children's Concert in 1957.

Six years later, at the age of 16, he made his first appearance with Leonard Bernstein and the New York Philharmonic in a nationally televised Young People's Concert. So impressed was the conductor with the young musician that only weeks later he asked Watts to replace the indisposed Glenn Gould at a regularly scheduled concert. Watts had barely two days' notice before reprising Franz Liszt's Concerto No. 2 in E-flat.

To be exposed to the world stage in such a fashion could have spelled disaster for a young musician. Watts, however, received a standing ovation, and suddenly found himself an international celebrity. Not content to bask in the applause, he decided to immerse himself in study with the fine pianist Leon Fleisher, with whom he remained for more than a decade. The onetime prodigy evolved into a mature artist who today, four decades after his auspicious debut, is one of the leading musicians of our time.

Born in Nuremberg, Germany, to a career soldier in the U.S. Army and a pianist mother, André Watts moved with his family to Philadelphia, where he studied at the Philadelphia Musical Academy (now University of the Arts). He later attended the Conservatory of Johns Hopkins University.

Watts excels in the grand-scale Romantic piano literature of composers such as Tchaikovsky, Chopin, Saint-Saëns, Franck, and the American Edward MacDowell, whose Piano Concerto No. 2 he plays to great acclaim. He also interprets, with probing insight, the more introspective and intimate repertoire, notably that of Schubert.

Critics pull out all stops in praising this remarkable pianist. They refer to his "formidable technical arsenal [and] still more-powerful intellect," his "thunderous power [and] flame-throwing virtuosity," "his insights, exquisitely penetrating and detailed," his "restraint and fluid grace," his "unearthly luminescence." One reviewer notes that Watts has "ten of the most dexterous digits ever to command a keyboard," and another has recalled what was perhaps the greatest audience tribute of all: total rapt silence after Watts played his own transcription of a Bach chorale prelude.

Perhaps most important is the fact that everything Watts does is in service of music, not showmanship. He has no onstage mannerisms, but plays in a straightforward manner that, to some, recalls the great Arthur Rubinstein.

Watts plays up to 100 concerts a year in every corner of the world with the world's greatest orchestras, among them the London, Boston, and Chicago Symphony Orchestras, as well as Japan's NHK and Tokyo Symphony Orchestras. Since his youthful debut at the Academy of Music, he has enjoyed a long and loyal relationship with The Philadelphian Orchestra, culminating in his appearance in 2000 at the ensemble's internationally telecast 100th Anniversary Gala Concert. He has appeared at Ravinia, Saratoga, Tanglewood, Mostly Mozart, Interlochen, and the Hollywood Bowl, and also gives many solo recitals. This past season Watts premiered an orchestral version of Schubert's *Fantasie in F minor*, which he commissioned.

André Watts has some of the most extensive television credits among classical musicians, including many guest appearances on PBS's *Live from Lincoln Center* series. His initial PBS Sunday afternoon telecast in 1976 was the first full-length piano recital in the history of television. Watts also appeared on PBS with the Mostly Mozart Festival Orchestra, and with the Chamber Music Society of Lincoln Center. At the latter's 30th Anniversary Gala in 1998, he served both as host and guest artist.

Watts's recorded works are many, notably the large romantic concertos with which his name is synonymous. He has also done solo recordings devoted to Chopin and to Schubert. Watts is included in the recently released Philips series, *Great Pianists of the 20th Century*.

At age 26, Watts was the youngest person ever to receive an honorary doctorate from Yale University, followed by similar honors from the University of Pennsylvania, Brandeis University, Juilliard School of Music, and the Peabody Conservatory, from which he also received a Distinguished Alumni Award. In 1988, he won the prestigious Avery Fisher Prize. In the 2000–2001 season he became Artist-in-Residence at the University of Maryland. A much-honored artist internationally, Watts has played before royalty in Europe and heads of government around the world.

DENYCE GRAVES

In the mid-1980s, *USA Today* had already declared the young mezzo-soprano Denyce Graves a likely operatic superstar for the 21st century. That prediction has come true. Graves is now one of the reigning divas of our day, sought by the world's leading opera houses, especially for sultry roles such as the gypsy heroine of Bizet's *Carmen*.

It was in that role that Graves made her 1995 debut at the Metropolitan Opera, her portrayal meshing a playful, bright craftiness with dark foreboding. The following season, she starred in the Met's new Franco Zeffirelli production of *Carmen*, and also reprised the role on opening night 1997. She has since taken Carmen to the world's major opera houses, including Covent Garden in London and the Bastille in Paris.

Another of Graves's signature roles is Dalila in Saint-Saëns's *Samson et Dalila*. She made her first appearance in this work with The Washington Opera at the Ravinia Festival under the direction of James Levine, later singing Dalila in a new Metropolitan Opera production and at Los Angeles Opera. In all three she appeared opposite renowned Spanish tenor Plácido Domingo. Domingo first met Graves at Houston Grand Opera, and the two have appeared together many times over the years. They are a glamorous duo that is hard to match on the operatic stage for sheer electricity.

Graves is a highly versatile artist. She has some 40 characterizations in her operatic repertoire, ranging from the heroine Charlotte in Massenet's tragic *Werther* to the High Priestess in Spontini's *La vestale*, which she sang in her La Scala debut (and which is now available on Sony Classical). Her comedic skills are highly developed, as she has demonstrated in roles such as Baba the Turk, the bearded lady in Stravinsky's *The Rake's Progress*, and the pert Dorabella in *Così fan tutte*, her first venture into the Mozartean repertoire. The latter performance was at the Opera Company of Philadelphia, a Resident

Company of the Academy of Music, which discovered Graves early in her career and this season presents the singer in her role debut as the heroine in Offenbach's sparkling operetta *La Périchole*.

Graves's magnetic stage presence and glowing voice have also brought her acclaim on the symphonic and recital stage. She has been soloist in masterworks such as Verdi's *Requiem Mass*, Handel's *Messiah*, and Rossini's *Stabat Mater*, infusing her interpretations with deep religious feeling. She has appeared with the world's leading orchestras, led by such renowned conductors as James Levine, Riccardo Muti, Zubin Mehta, Christoph Eschenbach, and Riccardo Chailly. As a recitalist she performs throughout the country, often with longtime accompanist Warren Jones at the piano. Her audiences demand encore after encore, reveling in her operatic and art song repertoire as well as selections from Broadway musicals, spirituals, crossover, and jazz.

Graves has been featured in two Emmy Award–winning television shows: CBS's *60 Minutes*, which profiled her career; and the BBC special "The Royal Opera House," which documented her debut performances there. Her discography includes French arias, spirituals, Christmas music, and operas. She was a soloist in Philip Glass's Symphony No. 5, released by Nonesuch in 2000.

PHOTO BY PHILIP BERMINGHAM

Denyce Graves grew up in Washington, D.C., raised by a strong and loving mother. By the fourth grade she was enamored of the world-renowned contralto and humanist Marian Anderson, who has remained a lifelong inspiration. In 1990, Graves had the honor of receiving the prestigious Marian Anderson Award from the legendary singer herself, then 88 years of age.

Graves attended the Duke Ellington High School for the Performing Arts, the Oberlin Conservatory of Music, and the New England Conservatory of Music. After a brief stint doing secretarial work, Graves was offered her first lead by Houston Grand Opera: the child Gretel in Humperdinck's beloved opera *Hansel and Gretel*. Singing was the easy part; she had to perform on roller skates.

Since then it has been a heady climb for the singer, who maintains a strong commitment to service, providing benefit performances for many causes. Her awards have been many, including an honorary doctorate from Oberlin. In 1999, WQXR Radio in New York City named Denyce Graves one of classical music's "Standard-Bearers for the 21st Century."

FREDERICA VON STADE

Known to family, friends, and fans by her nickname "Flicka," the slim, elegant mezzo-soprano Frederica von Stade has enriched the world of classical music for three decades. Her radiant, silver-hued voice of unusually large range is joined by a deep emotional sensibility, and her repertoire covers 400 years, from Monteverdi to contemporary works.

For many years, von Stade virtually owned the so-called "trouser roles"—operatic characterizations of boys and young men, particularly those in the throes of adolescent love, which require a light but full mezzo-soprano voice and a lithe figure. Von Stade fit the bill perfectly, and her vocal and dramatic skills consistently charmed audiences. Of her roles in this genre, her greatest was probably that of Cherubino in Mozart's *The Marriage of Figaro,* which she has performed around the world, from the Met to Glyndebourne, from San Francisco to the Paris Opera. Another audience favorite was her portrayal of Octavian in Richard Strauss's *Der Rosenkavalier.*

Von Stade has also developed a particular affinity for 19th-century French heroines, notably Claude Debussy's fragile Mélisande in the opera *Pelléas et Mélisande.* According to one critic, she is "the Mélisande of one's dreams," and she has said that this role is her all-time favorite. Other French characterizations have included Massenet's Cendrillon (Cinderella) and Béatrice in Berlioz's *Béatrice et Bénédict.* A bel canto specialist with a marvelous legato line and crystalline coloratura, von Stade made her memorable Covent Garden debut in 1975 as Rosina in *The Barber of Seville,* also mastering other difficult Rossini roles, including Desdemona in *Otello.*

In January 2000, von Stade took on the title role in Franz Lehár's *The Merry Widow* with the Metropolitan Opera, a production created specifically to celebrate her 30 years with the company. In the role of the enchanting widow Hannah, von Stade displayed what *Opera News* described as a spirit of "warmth, grace and class." The same year, in the San Francisco Opera's world premiere of Jake Heggie and Terrence McNally's *Dead Man Walking,* she transformed a minor role into the

heart of the opera, through her memorable portrait of a condemned killer's mother trying to come to grips with her son's heinous crime.

Many worthy but neglected operas have been revived for von Stade, including Jules Massenet's *Chérubin,* Ambroise Thomas's *Mignon,* and Claudio Monteverdi's *Il ritorno d'Ulisse in patria.* Among the gifted contemporary composers who have written operas with von Stade in mind are Dominick Argento and Conrad Susa. Von Stade created the role of Tina in Argento's *Aspern Papers* with the Dallas Opera, and the role of Madame de Merteuil in Susa's *Dangerous Liaisons* with the San Francisco Opera. Both world premieres were broadcast throughout North America.

Von Stade is a familiar presence on the concert stage, where she appears with the world's finest orchestras and conductors. She is frequently sought for her interpretations of Mozart, Mahler, Berlioz, Ravel, and Canteloube. On the recital stage, her vocal beauty, aristocratic bearing, emotional directness, and clarity of tone and diction are displayed in a broad repertoire that moves from old Italian airs to songs by Jerome Kern and Richard Rodgers, from the classical Haydn to the contemporary William Bolcom. Von Stade's longtime accompanist is the eminent pianist Martin Katz.

Heggie, the composer of *Dead Man Walking,* also set to music some of von Stade's own poems, including a cycle called "Paper Wings," which commemorates the singer's childhood and that of her daughters. Von Stade's father was killed in action at the end of World War II, just weeks before the singer's birth. He was memorialized by composer Richard Danielpour, who, in 1998, helped her to realize an artistic and personal dream when he wrote *Elegies,* scored for orchestra, mezzo-soprano, and baritone. The cycle, based on letters Mr. von Stade sent to his wife during the war, was recorded and released by Sony Classical.

Von Stade's more than three dozen recordings, including operas, arias, symphonic works, solo recitals, and popular crossover albums, have won numerous awards and citations, including the highest recording prizes in Germany, France, and Italy.

A New Jersey native, Frederica von Stade has been appointed an officer of L'Ordre des Arts et des Lettres by the French government and has been honored by the White House for her contribution to the arts. She holds several honorary doctorates, including one from her alma mater, the Mannes School of Music.

WARREN JONES

Pianist Warren Jones is one of the most sought-after collaborating musical artists in the world. His recitals with many of the greatest singers have inspired critics to describe him as "the singer's sympathetic soulmate," "the perfect musical partner," and "the single finest accompanist now working."

In addition to performing with this evening's mezzo-sopranos Denyce Graves and Frederica von Stade, Jones has appeared in concert with such stars as Marilyn Horne, Carol Vaness, Dame Kiri Te Kanawa, Samuel Ramey, Matti Talvela, and James Morris, and he has appeared on television with Luciano Pavarotti. Jones's efforts as both performer and teacher received national attention when he was profiled on *CBS Sunday Morning*.

Warren Jones has been a guest artist at Carnegie Hall and in Lincoln Center's Great Performers Series, as well as the Tanglewood, Ravinia, and Caramoor festivals, and he has been invited to perform at the White House on three occasions. His appearance at the United Nations memorial concert and tribute to the beloved actress Audrey Hepburn was telecast worldwide.

Among Jones's many CDs are a recording of spirituals with Denyce Graves and a collaboration with Samuel Ramey of Aaron Copland and Charles Ives songs, which was nominated for a Grammy Award. His memorable concert at the Metropolitan Museum of Art with soprano Kathleen Battle became a best-selling video/laser disc.

Education occupies a key role in Warren Jones's life. He is a member of the faculty of the Manhattan School of Music in New York City, where he mentors gifted young artists seeking a graduate degree in collaborative piano. He teaches and performs each summer at the Music Academy of the West in Santa Barbara, California. Jones is a prominent musical jurist at leading international competitions. He has received the Outstanding Alumni Award from the New England Conservatory of Music.

SIR ELTON JOHN

The monumental career of international singer/songwriter and performer Sir Elton John has spanned more than three decades. One of the top-selling solo artists of all time, he has won countless awards, including Grammys, Tonys, and an Oscar, and can boast 34 gold and 24 platinum albums. Combining flamboyant costumes and electrifying onstage performances with a rich voice and superb songwriting, John has delighted audiences from London to Los Angeles to the former U.S.S.R.

As a songwriter, his gifts have never been more compelling than on the soundtrack for Disney's 1994 blockbuster *The Lion King*, for which John and lyricist Tim Rice received an Academy Award for best original song, "Can You Feel the Love Tonight?" For the same song, John won a Grammy in the Best Male Pop Vocal category. That same year, he was inducted into the Rock and Roll Hall of Fame. John and Rice teamed up again in 2000 for the rock musical *Aida*, based on the Verdi opera of that name, winning a Grammy Award for best musical show album.

Born Reginald Dwight in Pinner, Middlesex, England, the future pop star began playing piano at the age of four, and by 11 he'd won a scholarship to the Royal Academy of Music. While at the Academy, he performed with several rock bands and formed his own R&B group, Bluesology. After leaving the Academy, he toured England with Bluesology, played piano in hotels, and worked for a music publisher.

In 1967 Dwight linked up with lyricist Bernard Taupin to form a professional songwriting team. Taking the stage name Elton "Hercules" John, he began his solo career in 1968, singing songs he'd written with Taupin. The 1970 album *Elton John*, featuring the classic "Your Song," made him a star in the United Kingdom and launched his career in

the United States, where he toured that year. He and Taupin produced several more albums together, including *Honky Chateau*, John's first No. 1 album, which contained the smash hit "Rocket Man." This started a string of successes for the entertainer, who scored 16consecutive Top 20 Hits in the 1970s. Elton John not only topped Elvis Presley with the most consecutive years of *Billboard* Top 40 hits, he also became the only artist to reach the Top 30 for 23 uninterrupted years.

In 1980 John and Taupin, who had ceased working together in the late '70s, reunited for *21 at 33*. In 1981, John signed with Geffen Records, and he continued to produce gold albums throughout the 1980s, including 1983's *Too Low for Zero*, featuring "I'm Still Standing" and "I Guess That's Why They Call It the Blues." His 1995 album, *Made in England*, reunited him with the acclaimed arranger Paul Buckmaster (with whom he had worked on *Elton John*) and scaled the charts throughout the world.

In 1997, following the tragic death of his friend, Princess Diana, Elton John was asked by her family to sing at her funeral in Westminster Abbey. His performance was seen by an estimated 2 billion people worldwide, and his poignant tribute, "Candle in the Wind," quickly became the best-selling single of all time, with some 32 million copies in distribution. John designated that money from the sales go to a fund established in the Princess's memory.

His latest album, *Songs from the West Coast*, was released by Universal Records in October 2001.

Elton John has given generously to many philanthropic causes, including the fight against AIDS. His AIDS foundation, headquartered in Atlanta, has awarded grants totaling more than $5 million worldwide for education, research, and patient care, making it one of the largest nonprofit organizations in the fight against this disease. The self-confessed "shopaholic" placed 10,000 outfits from his wardrobe on sale to raise money for the foundation. He also donates royalties from his singles to AIDS charities. For his many philanthropic activities, Elton John was knighted by Queen Elizabeth II in 1998.

Sir Elton John's ties to Philadelphia relate not only to his appearances here over the years, but also to his single "Philadelphia Freedom," which he wrote for tennis pro and friend Billie Jean King. King was in Denver, coaching her Philadelphia Freedoms tennis team in a playoff game, when Elton John visited the locker room with a tape recorder and played his song for her. King loved it, as did the rest of the nation. Released in March 1975, the record went gold in April. ∎

Saturday evening, December 15, 7:00 P.M.

VERIZON HALL • PHILADELPHIA ORCHESTRA INAUGURAL CONCERT

THE PHILADELPHIA ORCHESTRA

WOLFGANG SAWALLISCH, *CONDUCTOR*

EMANUEL AX, PIANO

ITZHAK PERLMAN, VIOLIN

YO-YO MA, CELLO

THE PHILADELPHIA SINGERS CHORALE

(DAVID HAYES, MUSIC DIRECTOR)

JOHN STAFFORD SMITH (1750–1836)	THE STAR SPANGLED BANNER (ORCHESTRATED BY EUGENE ORMANDY)
AARON JAY KERNIS (B. 1960)	COLOR WHEEL—WORLD PREMIERE PERFORMANCE (COMMISSIONED BY THE PHILADELPHIA ORCHESTRA FOR THE OPENING OF ITS NEW HOME AT THE KIMMEL CENTER)
LUDWIG VAN BEETHOVEN (1770–1827)	TRIPLE CONCERTO IN C MAJOR, OP. 56 (FOR PIANO, VIOLIN, CELLO, AND ORCHESTRA) 1. ALLEGRO 2. LARGO 3. RONDO ALLA POLACCA—ALLEGRO—TEMPO I
MAURICE RAVEL (1875–1937)	SUITE NO. 2 FROM *DAPHNIS AND CHLOÉ* (FOR LARGE ORCHESTRA AND WORDLESS CHORUS) DAYBREAK—PANTOMIME—GENERAL DANCE

The world premiere of *Color Wheel* is made possible in part by grants from the National Endowment for the Arts and the Philadelphia Music Project (funded by The Pew Charitable Trusts and administered by the Philadelphia Settlement Music School). | Through the support of a group of generous corporations and individuals, this concert is being broadcast live via WHYY television and radio and made available worldwide via the Internet through *andante.com* and *whyy.org*. | Lexus is the exclusive automotive sponsor of The Philadelphia Orchestra.

THE PHILADELPHIA ORCHESTRA | 2001–2002 SEASON

WOLFGANG SAWALLISCH, Music Director, *Walter and Leonore Annenberg Endowed Chair*
Rossen Milanov, Assistant Conductor | **Luis Biava**, Conductor in Residence

FIRST VIOLINS

DAVID KIM, CONCERTMASTER
Dr. Benjamin Rush Endowed Chair

WILLIAM DE PASQUALE,
  CO-CONCERTMASTER

MICHAEL LUDWIG,
  ASSOCIATE CONCERTMASTER

NANCY BEAN,
  ASSISTANT CONCERTMASTER

HERBERT LIGHT

BARBARA GOVATOS

LARRY GRIKA

HEROLD KLEIN

VLADIMIR SHAPIRO

JONATHAN BEILER

ARNOLD GROSSI

HIRONO OKA

RICHARD AMOROSO

YAYOI NUMAZAWA

JASON DEPUE

LAURA PARK

LISA-BETH LAMBERT

SECOND VIOLINS

KIMBERLY FISHER, PRINCIPAL

PAUL ROBY,
  ASSOCIATE PRINCIPAL

JOSEPH LANZA,
  ASSISTANT PRINCIPAL

PHILIP KATES

VIRGINIA HALFMANN

LOUIS LANZA

STEPHANE DALSCHAERT

BOOKER ROWE

DAVYD BOOTH

PAUL ARNOLD

YUMI NINOMIYA SCOTT

DMITRI LEVIN

BORIS BALTER

JEROME WIGLER

VIOLAS

ROBERTO DÍAZ, PRINCIPAL

CHOONG-JIN CHANG,
  ASSOCIATE PRINCIPAL

SIDNEY CURTISS,
  ASSISTANT PRINCIPAL

JUDY GEIST

LEONARD BOGDANOFF

ALBERT FILOSA

DONALD R. CLAUSER

RENARD EDWARDS

ANNA MARIE AHN PETERSEN

STEPHEN WYRCZYNSKI

DAVID NICASTRO

BURCHARD TANG

CHE-HUNG CHEN

CELLOS

WILLIAM STOKKING, PRINCIPAL
*Albert and Mildred Switky
Endowed Chair*

PETER STUMPF,
  ASSOCIATE PRINCIPAL

LLOYD SMITH,
  ASSISTANT PRINCIPAL

RICHARD HARLOW

GLORIA DE PASQUALE

KATHRYN PICHT READ

ROBERT CAFARO

OHAD BAR-DAVID

JOHN KOEN

JOHN HAINES-EITZEN

DEREK BARNES

ALEX VELTMAN

BASSES

HAROLD ROBINSON, PRINCIPAL

MICHAEL SHAHAN,
  ASSOCIATE PRINCIPAL

NEIL COURTNEY,
  ASSISTANT PRINCIPAL

JOHN HOOD

EMILIO GRAVAGNO

HENRY G. SCOTT

DAVID FAY

DUANE ROSENGARD

ROBERT KESSELMAN

*Some members of the string
sections voluntarily rotate seating
on a periodic basis.*

FLUTES

JEFFREY KHANER, PRINCIPAL

DAVID CRAMER,
  ASSOCIATE PRINCIPAL

LOREN N. LIND

KAZUO TOKITO, PICCOLO

OBOES

RICHARD WOODHAMS,
  PRINCIPAL
Samuel S. Fels Endowed Chair

PETER SMITH,
  ASSOCIATE PRINCIPAL

JONATHAN BLUMENFELD

ELIZABETH STARR MASOUDNIA,
  ENGLISH HORN

CLARINETS

SAMUEL CAVIEZEL, PRINCIPAL
Volunteer Committees Endowed Chair

DONALD MONTANARO,
  ASSOCIATE PRINCIPAL

RAOUL QUERZE

RONALD REUBEN,
  BASS CLARINET

BASSOONS

DANIEL MATSUKAWA, PRINCIPAL

MARK GIGLIOTTI, CO-PRINCIPAL

ANGELA ANDERSON

HOLLY BLAKE, CONTRABASSOON

HORNS

NOLAN MILLER, PRINCIPAL

DAVID WETHERILL,
  CO-PRINCIPAL

DANIEL WILLIAMS

JEFFRY KIRSCHEN

ADAM UNSWORTH

SHELLEY SHOWERS

TRUMPETS

DAVID BILGER, PRINCIPAL

JEFFREY CURNOW,
  ASSOCIATE PRINCIPAL

ROBERT W. EARLEY

ROGER BLACKBURN

TROMBONES

NITZAN HAROZ, PRINCIPAL

MATTHEW VAUGHN,
  ASSOCIATE PRINCIPAL

ERIC CARLSON

BLAIR BOLLINGER,
  BASS TROMBONE

TUBA

PAUL KRZYWICKI

TIMPANI

DON S. LIUZZI, PRINCIPAL
Dwight V. Dowley Endowed Chair

MICHAEL BOOKSPAN,
  ASSOCIATE PRINCIPAL

ANGELA ZATOR NELSON

PERCUSSION

MICHAEL BOOKSPAN, PRINCIPAL

ANTHONY ORLANDO

ANGELA ZATOR NELSON

PIANO AND CELESTA

KIYOKO TAKEUTI

HARPS

ELIZABETH HAINEN DEPETERS,
  PRINCIPAL

MARGARITA CSONKA
  MONTANARO, CO-PRINCIPAL

LIBRARIANS

CLINTON F. NIEWEG, PRINCIPAL

ROBERT M. GROSSMAN

NANCY M. BRADBURD

STAGE PERSONNEL

EDWARD BARNES, MANAGER

JAMES J. SWEENEY, JR.

JAMES P. BARNES

ABOUT THE ARTISTS

WOLFGANG SAWALLISCH

Music Director, The Philadelphia Orchestra

Walter and Leonore Annenberg Endowed Chair

PHOTO BY
PETER CHECCHIA

The 2001–2002 season marks Wolfgang Sawallisch's ninth year as Music Director of The Philadelphia Orchestra. Acclaimed as one of the greatest living exponents of the Germanic musical tradition, he has enriched and expanded upon the Orchestra's century-old tradition of excellence. Mr. Sawallisch has re-affirmed The Philadelphia Orchestra's commitment to new music through a series of ongoing commissions. His vision for the Orchestra's 100th Anniversary Season in 1999–2000, made up exclusively from music written since the ensemble's creation in 1900, resulted in record ticket sales and critical praise. His concert tours with the Orchestra have included performances on four continents, from Beijing to Birmingham, from Buenos Aires to Boston.

Throughout his tenure, Mr. Sawallisch has been an outspoken advocate for the construction of The Philadelphia Orchestra's new home at The Kimmel Center for the Performing Arts. He has actively participated in planning for the new concert hall's acoustics and its operations, and he conducts the Orchestra's first performances in the Center's Verizon Hall at the Gala Preview Concert on December 14 and in the Orchestra's Gala Inaugural Concert on December 15.

Mr. Sawallisch has encouraged the exploration of new ways to present music to American audiences. In April 1997, he led the Philadelphians in the first live Internet concert "cybercast" made by a major American orchestra, attracting listeners from more than 40 countries around the world. He has presented season-long focuses on the works of Haydn, Beethoven, and Brahms, and an ongoing overview of the works of Richard Strauss (including a concert presentation of the opera *Ariadne auf Naxos*). In February 1994, for a concert he was to conduct, he stepped in alone to replace the entire Orchestra (snowed-in at various points throughout the city) for an extraordinary evening of Wagnerian opera highlights, accompanying the scheduled soloists and chorus on piano.

Since becoming music director in 1993, Wolfgang Sawallisch has led The Philadelphia Orchestra each year in concerts outside Philadelphia, helping to build upon the ensemble's long tradition of touring. They appear together annually in a series of concerts at Carnegie Hall and have performed in major concert halls throughout the world on eight international tours (three to Europe, four to Asia, and one to Central and South America). Earlier this fall, they completed a triumphant concert tour across the United States, performing 12 concerts in nine states.

Wolfgang Sawallisch was born in Munich and graduated from that city's Academy of Music. He began his conducting career in 1947 at the Opera Theater of Augsburg, where he served as vocal coach, chorus master, and conductor of ballet, opera, and concert music. In 1953 he became the youngest conductor to lead the Berlin Philharmonic, an orchestra with which he is associated to this day. He next held successive music directorships in Aachen, Wiesbaden, and Cologne and appeared annually at the prestigious Bayreuth Festival. He was music director of the Vienna Symphony 1960–70, and he also served as music director of the Hamburg Philharmonic 1963–71. He served as artistic director of Geneva's Orchestre de la Suisse Romande 1973–80. In 1971 he was appointed music director of the Bavarian State Opera in Munich, beginning an exceptionally fruitful and long-lasting relationship with that company. Working in Munich for more than two decades, he served concurrently as the Opera's general manager during his last ten years there before coming to Philadelphia.

As a guest conductor, Mr. Sawallisch leads concerts each year with the Vienna Symphony and Tokyo's NHK Orchestra. Other recent guest appearances include performances with the Berlin Philharmonic, Vienna Philharmonic, Orchestre de Paris, Israel Philharmonic, London's Philharmonia, and the Czech Philharmonic.

Mr. Sawallisch's extensive discography includes a wide range of orchestral and opera recordings, both with The Philadelphia Orchestra and with a number of European ensembles. His recordings of Robert Schumann's symphonies with the Dresden Staatskapelle on the EMI label are often considered a benchmark against which other conductors' renditions are measured. His Philadelphia compact discs include works by Bruckner, Dvořák, Hindemith, and Tchaikovsky, as well as a special disc of orchestral transcriptions by Leopold Stokowski and a four-disc cycle of the orchestral works of Richard Strauss.

Wolfgang Sawallisch is highly regarded as a chamber musician and accompanist. He has collaborated and recorded with such vocalists as Dietrich Fischer-Dieskau, Hermann Prey, Peter Schreier, and Margaret Price, as well as with the Munich Residenz Quartet. His most recent recordings as a pianist include Schubert's *Winterreise* and Schumann songs with Thomas Hampson, and a disc of 20th-century works with trumpeter Ole Edvard Antonsen. He often performs with members of The Philadelphia Orchestra, appearing frequently on the Orchestra's annual Chamber Music Series.

Mr. Sawallisch's artistry has been recognized throughout his career with many awards and citations. He was given the Toscanini Gold Baton in recognition of his 35-year association with La Scala in Milan. His honorary degrees include a doctorate from the Curtis Institute of Music in Philadelphia.

EMANUEL AX

Pianist Emanuel Ax is renowned not only for his poetic temperament and unsurpassed virtuosity, but also for the exceptional breadth of his performing activity. Each season his distinguished career includes appearances with major symphony orchestras worldwide, recitals in the most celebrated concert halls, a variety of chamber music collaborations, the commissioning and performance of new music, and additions to his acclaimed discography.

PHOTO BY J. HENRY FAIR

Emanuel Ax first captured public attention in 1974 when, at age 25, he won the first Arthur Rubinstein International Piano Competition in Tel Aviv. He made his debut with The Philadelphia Orchestra a year later, at the Robin Hood Dell with guest conductor Michael Tilson Thomas. Additional awards and engagements with other leading orchestras soon followed, quickly advancing and promoting the young artist's expanding international career. In 1979 he was awarded the prestigious Avery Fisher Award.

Devoted to chamber music literature, Mr. Ax regularly collaborates with such artists as Young Uck Kim, Jaime Laredo, Cho-Liang Lin, Yo-Yo Ma, Peter Serkin, and Isaac Stern. Mr. Ax has toured extensively in recent seasons with Isaac Stern, Jaime Laredo, and Yo-Yo Ma.

An exceptional and compelling recording artist, Mr. Ax has recorded exclusively for Sony Classical since 1987. His extensive discography encompasses a diverse repertoire of orchestral and chamber works in collaboration with many distinguished conductors, orchestras, and instrumentalists, as well as acclaimed solo albums, featuring music ranging from Brahms to Piazzolla, and from Beethoven and Chopin to Corigliano and Adams. Mr. Ax's recent releases have included a

Grammy Award–winning album of Haydn Piano Sonatas, a two-disc set of period-instrument performances of Chopin's complete works for piano and orchestra, three solo Brahms albums, and the Brahms Concerto No. 2 with the Boston Symphony. His chamber music recordings in collaboration with many distinguished artists have been widely acclaimed. As a duo, Ax and Yo-Yo Ma were awarded three Grammy Awards for their performances of the Beethoven and Brahms sonatas for cello and piano.

During the past decade, Mr. Ax has turned increasing attention to performing new works and nurturing the creativity of living composers, performing works by such diverse figures as William Bolcolm, Peter Lieberson, Ezra Laderman, Paul Hindemith, Hans Werner Henze, André Previn, Michael Tippett, and Joseph Schwanter. He also has been instrumental in commissioning a series of new concertos, premiering *Century Rolls* by John Adams in 1997, *Seeing* by Christopher Rouse in 1999, *Red Silk Dance* by Bright Sheng in 2000, and, with The Philadelphia Orchestra, a new concerto by Krzysztof Penderecki in 2002. His commitment to establishing these new works in the repertoire was demonstrated by numerous subsequent performances of *Century Rolls* with orchestras throughout Europe and North America, including here in Philadelphia, as well as a recording with the Cleveland Orchestra.

Since his debut with The Philadelphia Orchestra in 1975, Mr. Ax has returned to play with the ensemble on many occasions, most recently in March 2001.

Born in Lvov, Poland, Emanuel Ax began playing the violin at age six. He soon changed to piano, studying with his father, a coach at the Lvov Opera House. The Ax family moved to Winnipeg, Canada, when Emanuel was a young boy, and several years later they settled in New York. As a student of Mieczylaw Munz, Emanuel Ax enrolled in the pre-college division of the Juilliard School of Music.

Mr. Ax is a graduate of Columbia University, where he majored in French. He lives in New York City with his wife, pianist Yoko Nozaki, their son, Joseph, and their daughter, Sarah.

ITZHAK PERLMAN

Itzhak Perlman enjoys a superstar status rarely afforded to classical musicians. Equally at ease on the concert stage, the sets of television programs from *Sesame Street* to *Live from Lincoln Center*, and in the classroom, violinist Itzhak Perlman has captured the hearts of music lovers everywhere. He is recognized throughout the world for his superb artistry, the irrepressible joy of his music-making, and the deep personal sense of humanity inherent in everything he does.

Born in Israel in 1945, Itzhak Perlman completed his initial training at the Academy of Music in Tel Aviv. His talents were recognized early and he was soon performing in recital, with orchestra, and on state radio programs. He came to New York and was subsequently propelled into the public eye through an appearance on the *Ed Sullivan Show* in 1958. Following studies at the Juilliard School of Music with Ivan Galamian and Dorothy DeLay, Mr. Perlman won the prestigious Leventritt International Competition in 1964, which quickly fueled his burgeoning international career.

PHOTO BY
AKIRA KINOSHITA

Today, Itzhak Perlman performs more than 100 concerts annually, in recital and with orchestras throughout the world. He has played with all the major orchestras of North America, and has made concert tours of Australia, the Far East, Europe, and South America. In the spring of 1990, he joined the Israel Philharmonic in their historic first concert tour to the Soviet Union, and, in December 1990, he returned to Leningrad (now St. Petersburg) for a celebration concert honoring the 150th anniversary of Tchaikovsky's birth, joining cellist Yo-Yo Ma, soprano Jessye Norman, and the Leningrad Philharmonic under the direction of Yuri Temirkanov.

During the past several seasons, Mr. Perlman has devoted some of his creative energies to conducting, appearing with many of this country's leading ensembles, including annual summer performances with The Philadelphia Orchestra. This fall, he assumed new responsibilities as principal guest conductor of the Detroit Symphony Orchestra.

Mr. Perlman's recordings—for nearly every major label—encompass the greater part of the violin literature, and include several award-winning performances often cited as definitive interpretations. His compact discs regularly appear on the best-seller charts and have won 15 Grammy Awards. His most recent releases have included two albums featuring popular hits from movies (with John Williams conducting the Pittsburgh Symphony and Boston Pops Orchestra), and a recording of Brahms's Double Concerto (with Yo-Yo Ma and the Chicago Symphony). In 1995 EMI honored Mr. Perlman on the occasion of his 50th birthday with the release of a 21-CD set entitled *The Itzhak Perlman Collection*.

Mr. Perlman's presence on stage, on camera, and in personal appearances speaks eloquently on behalf of the handicapped and disabled—Mr. Perlman had polio at the age of four—and his devotion to this cause is an integral part of his life. Among his proudest achievements was his collaboration with film score composer John Williams in Steven Speilberg's Academy Award–winning film *Schindler's List*, in which he performed the violin solos.

Itzhak Perlman made his debut with The Philadelphia Orchestra in April 1965, at the age of 20, and has returned frequently to play with the Orchestra. In 1999 he made his conducting debut with the Orchestra, and has encored this role annually since that time, leading a concert this past summer during the Orchestra's annual summer residency at the Mann Center in Philadelphia's Fairmount Park.

YO-YO MA

The many-faceted career of cellist Yo-Yo Ma is testament to his continual search for new ways to communicate with audiences, and to his personal desire for artistic growth and renewal. Whether performing a new concerto, revisiting a familiar work, coming together with colleagues for chamber music, reaching out to young audiences and student musicians, or exploring culture and musical forms outside of the Western classical tradition, Mr. Ma strives to find connections that stimulate the imagination.

Today, as one of the most sought-after cellists, Yo-Yo Ma regularly appears with eminent conductors and leading orchestras throughout the world. He maintains a careful balance among his various engagements—as concerto soloist, collaborative chamber musician, solo recitalist, and artistic catalyst. One of Mr. Ma's personal and career goals is exploration of music as a means of communication and as a vehicle for the migration of ideas across a range of cultures throughout the world. To that end, he has taken time to immerse himself in subjects as diverse as native Chinese music and its distinctive instruments, or the music of the Kalahari bush people in Africa.

PHOTO BY J. HENRY FAIR

Taking his cross-cultural interests to new areas and audiences, Mr. Ma recently established the Silk Road Project to promote the study of artistic and intellectual traditions along the ancient Silk Road trade route, which extended from easternmost Asia to Europe (including India, Tibet, Persia, and Greece). By examining the ebb and flow of ideas throughout this vast area, the Project seeks to illuminate the heritages of the Silk Road countries and to identify the voices that represent these traditions today. This forward-looking project about past roots and traditions encompasses a variety of planned compact disc recordings and multimedia components, along with music commissions, live performances, and a special Web site.

Highly acclaimed for his ensemble playing, Mr. Ma regularly performs chamber music with a wide circle of colleagues, including Emanuel Ax, Daniel Barenboim, Christoph Eschenbach, Pamela Frank, Jeffrey Kahane, Young Uck Kim, Jaime Laredo, Peter Serkin, Isaac Stern, Richard Stoltzman, and Kathryn Stott.

Yo-Yo Ma works to expand the cello repertoire through performances of lesser-known music from the 20th century and the commissioning of new concertos and recital pieces. He has premiered works by a diverse group of composers, including pieces by Stephen Albert, William Bolcolm, Chen Qigang, Richard Danielpour, John Corigliano, John Harbison, Leon Kirchner, Christopher Rouse, Bright Sheng, Tan Dun, and John Williams.

Yo-Yo Ma is an exclusive Sony Classical recording artist, and his discography of nearly 50 albums (including 14 Grammy Award winners) is a direct reflection of his wide-ranging interests. In addition to the standard concerto repertoire, Mr. Ma has recorded many of the works he has commissioned or premiered. He has also made several successful recordings that defy simple categorization, including *Hush* with vocalist Bobby McFerrin, *Appalachia Waltz* with violinist Mark O'Connor and bassist Edgar Meyer, and *Piazzolla: Soul of the Tango*.

Yo-Yo Ma was born in 1955 to Chinese parents living in Paris. He studied principally with Leonard Rose at the Juilliard School, but also sought to expand his conservatory training through liberal arts studies at Harvard University. Mr. Ma and his wife, Jill, have two children, Nicholas and Emily.

Mr. Ma first appeared with The Philadelphia Orchestra in 1981 with guest conductor Andrew Davis. He has returned to play with the Orchestra on a regular basis since that time, most recently this past summer during the Orchestra's annual PNC Concert Series at the Mann Center for the Performing Arts.

Resident Chorus of The Philadelphia Orchestra
PHILADELPHIA SINGERS CHORALE
David Hayes, Music Director

The Philadelphia Singers Chorale was founded in 1991 as the symphonic chorus of the Philadelphia Singers. The Singers was created in 1972 by Michael Korn, who dedicated the group to presenting choral music of the highest caliber while offering challenging opportunities to professional singers. The expanded Singers Chorale is composed of professional singers and talented volunteers. David Hayes became music director in 1992.

Since its inception, The Philadelphia Singers Chorale has performed each season with The Philadelphia Orchestra and last year was named the Orchestra's resident chorus beginning with the 2001–2002 season. In addition to this evening's Inaugural Philadelphia Orchestra Concert in Verizon Hall, the Singers Chorale is joining with the Orchestra this season in performances of Handel's *Messiah*, MacMillan's *Quickening*, and Verdi's *Requiem*. Past collaborations with the Orchestra have included performances of Schoenberg's *Gurrelieder*, Liszt's *Dante Symphony*, Mahler's Second and Third symphonies, Brahms's *Requiem*, Haydn's *The Seasons*, Beethoven's Symphony No. 9 and "Choral" Fantasy, Adams's *Harmonium*, excerpts from Wagner's *Tannhäuser*, Honegger's *Jeanne d'Arc au bûcher*, and Prokofiev's *Ivan the Terrible*.

In addition to their work with The Philadelphia Orchestra, the Philadelphia Singers and Chorale present their own annual series of hometown concerts, as well as performing with other groups in Philadelphia and around the region. They regularly perform with the New York Philharmonic and have also collaborated in presentations with the Pennsylvania Ballet, Curtis Institute of Music, and the Chamber Orchestra of Philadelphia. The Philadelphia Singers have recorded three discs for RCA, including two Christmas recordings, *Gloria! Gloria!* and *Ceremonies of Carols*, and Handel's *Roman Vespers*.

David Hayes was appointed music director of the Philadelphia Singers in October 1992. He studied conducting with Charles Bruck at the Pierre Monteux School and with Otto-Werner Mueller at Curtis, where he is a staff conductor and faculty member. He also serves as head of orchestral conducting at New York's Mannes School of Music. In addition to his work in preparing a variety of choruses for performances, Mr. Hayes frequently appears as a guest conductor, including with the Los Angeles Master Chorale and Sinfonia Orchestra, the Chamber Orchestra of Philadelphia, Curtis Institute Symphony and Opera Theatre, Relâche Ensemble, Springfield Symphony, Louisiana Philharmonic, European Center for Opera and Vocal Art, Warsaw Philharmonic, American Repertory Ballet, Mendelssohn Choir of Pittsburgh, and at the Verbier and Berkshire Choral festivals.

THE KIMMEL CENTER

THE PHILADELPHIA SINGERS CHORALE

DAVID HAYES, Music Director

EMILIA ACON	PAULO FAUSTINI	JAMES KOURY	ALICIA ONDIK	JAN TAYLOR
IAN ALEXANDER	LISA FOLKERT	MICHAEL KRUEGER	JOHN OVERBECK	GINA TEAGUE
JANE ALLISON	THERESA FORSYTH	PAUL LAFOLLETTE	JAMES PALMER	REBECCA TEST
JOAN ANDERSON	JANE FOSTER	ROBERT LAIRD	HOLLY PHARES	NANCY TICE
MARK ANDERSON	MARIA FOX	LISA LANDLEY	FRANKLIN PHILLIPS	PAMELA TICE
JEAN ANDREOZZI	KATHERINE FRETZ	ROBERT LANDLEY	ROBERT PHILLIPS	GILL TIMON
DONNA APELDORN LEVIN	KAREN FUNG	CHERYL LAWRENCE	BRIAN PHIPPS	RICHARD TOLSMA
AMY ARMSTRONG	KENNETH GARNER	DONALD LAWRENCE	LOURIN PLANT	NANCY TRAUGER
CHRISTOPHER AUSTIN	TERI GEMBERLING-JOHNSON	LUISA LEHRER	NANCY PLUM	SALLIE VAN MERKENSTEIJN
LOIS BABBITT	BRENT GERHART	JOHN LEONARD	BOBBIE POTSIC	HEIDI VELHAGEN
BARBARA BALDWIN	DAWN GOOD	THOMAS LEVER	BONNIE POWELL	ELIZABETH WALKER
DAVID BANEY	WALTER GRANGER	HEATHER LOCKARD	DAVID PRICE	TOMMIE BORTON WARDER
STEPHEN BARSKY	CAROL GREY	JAMES LONGACRE	ANNA PULASKI	TERESA WASHAM
KAREN BLANCHARD	WILLIAM GREY	MICHAEL MAGIERA	EMILY REICH	MARY WEBB
MATTHEW DELLICH	KATHERINE GRUNDSTEIN	KATHERINE MALLON-DAY	SUSAN RHEINGANS	DEBORAH WEBSTER
PEGGI BREUNINGER	FRANK HAMPTON	FERNANDO MANCILLAS	CAMRON RUDNESMITH	ROLAND WEDGWOOD
ENNIO BRUGNOLO	ALYSON HARVEY	FAY MANICKE	KAREN RICHTER	JOHN WHITE
SHELLIE CAMP	FRANCIS HEALY	NANCY R. F. MARKS	M'ANNETTE RUDDELL	M.J. WHITEMAN
PETER CAMPBELL	ANDREW HEIMEL	JUDITH MARRACCINI	SARAH RUNNING	REBECCA WHITLOW
GREGORY CANTWELL	JOSEPH HEISE	ANDREW MASSO	JUDY RUSSO	HORACE WILLIAMS
RENEE CANTWELL	BARTON HENDERSON	LESLIE MAYRO	EVELYN SANTIAGO SCHULZ	ELIZABETH WITTER
MARCELLA CAPRARIO	MICHAEL HENDRICKS	JO MCDONALD	CANDACE SASSAMAN	LILA WOODRUFF MAY
DOROTHY CARDELLA	MICHAEL HENEISE	PAULINE MENSING	MICHAEL SAVINO	IVAN WOODS
SANDRA CARNEY	LAURIE HESS	BETSY MEREDITH	JOY SCHAUER	THOMAS WOODWARD
REBECCA CARR	CHRISTINA HODESS	CHARLES MEREDITH	MAURY SCHULTE	JOHN WRIGHT, JR.
WALT CARSON	CHRISTOPHER HODGES	ALLEN METZGER	RICK SCHWEIN	CHARLES WURSTER
CECELIA CHAISSON	ELIZABETH HOHWIELER	JOYCE MICHELFELDER	ROBYN SHAPIRO	RICHARD ZUCH
LYNDA CHEN	LOIS HUBER	MICHAEL MARTIN MILLS	ULRIKE SHAPIRO	
BRIAN CLANCY	JANE HULTING	FRANK MITCHELL	DAVID SHARP	LUKE HOUSNER, ACCOMPANIST
ELIZABETH COOK	LESLIE JACOBSON KAYE	DONLEROY MORALES	CAROL SHELLY	
KRYSTIANE COOPER	MARGARET JANKOWSKI	JANET MORAN	ESTHER SHISLER	JONATHAN COOPERSMITH, ASSISTANT CONDUCTOR & PERSONNEL MANAGER
MARK DAUGHERTY	STUART JASPER	CHARLES MORGAN	MARGARET SIPPLE	
DORALENE DAVIS	JANE JENNINGS	BETTY MORRELL	PETER SIPPLE	NANCY PLUM, VOLUNTEER COORDINATOR
JAMES DAVIS	ROBERT JOHNS	FRANK NARDI, SR.	JOHN SLIVON	
BELA DEBRECENI	STEPHEN JONES	CHRISTINE NASS	RUTH STARKEY	DAVID BANEY, EXECUTIVE DIRECTOR
ROBIN DEBRECENI	STACY KARAS	JOHN NELSON	JAMES STIEBER	
ROSS DRUKER	JESSICA KASINKSKI	TERESA NEVOLA	MARIAN STIEBER	ROBERT MORTENSEN, GENERAL MANAGER
DANIEL EAST	JOHN KENNEDY	ELIZABETH OLIVER	LESLIE SUDOCK	
LOUISE EVANS	BERT KORNFELD	TIMOTHY OLIVER	MARY ANN TANCREDI	

A B O U T   T H E   M U S I C

COLOR WHEEL

*commissioned by The Philadelphia Orchestra for the opening of
Verizon Hall at The Kimmel Center for the Performing Arts, and
premiered on December 15, 2001*

Aaron Jay Kernis

born in Philadelphia on January 15, 1960

*This work runs about 15 minutes in performance. Kernis has scored it for a
large ensemble comprised of 4 flutes (two doubling piccolos), 3 oboes (one
doubling English horn), 3 clarinets in b-flat (one doubling e-flat clarinet
and one doubling bass clarinet), 3 bassoons (one doubling contrabassoon),
4 horns, 3 trumpets in C (one doubling trumpet in D), 2 trombones,
bass trombone, tuba, timpani, a large array of percussion (including
glockenspiel, crotales, vibraphone, xylophone, marimba, chimes, tuned
gongs, water gong, almglocken, large crash cymbal, small hand cymbals,
suspended cymbals, tam-tams, triangles, bongos, piccolo snare drum, snare
drum, tom-toms, bass drums, woodblocks, castanets on a stick, and metal
shaker), electric bass, piano (doubling celesta), harp, and strings.
Groupings of additional brass (3 trumpets and 3 trombones) provide
antiphonal effects from points within the concert hall near the
conclusion of the work.*

The creation of Color Wheel *for the opening of the Orchestra's new home
at The Kimmel Center for the Performing Arts was made possible in part
by funding through grants from the National Endowment for the Arts and
the Philadelphia Music Project (funded by The Pew Charitable Trusts and
administered by the Philadelphia Settlement Music School).*

Color Wheel *is one of eight new works commissioned by The Philadelphia
Orchestra in celebration of its 100th anniversary in the year 2000 and premiered between November 1999 and June 2002.*

FROM THE COMPOSER:

The honor of being asked to write a piece to mark the opening of The
Philadelphia Orchestra's new concert hall led me to conceive of a
miniature "concerto for orchestra," treating it as a large and dynamic
body of sound and color. The work features the virtuosity of this
Orchestra's larger sections (winds, strings, brass, percussion) and to a
great extent focuses on distinct groups of instruments separately and in
combination rather than on individual soloists.

There were many experiences that helped to inspire the process of
writing this piece. Long before starting it, I met with architect
Rafael Viñoly and acoustician Russell Johnson to learn about the
development of the new hall. Shortly before that, I'd completed an
ambient sound score for the new Rose Center for Earth & Space at the
Museum of Natural History in New York, and was fascinated by the
challenge of writing for a specific acoustical environment.

Initially I'd intended that *Color Wheel* would explore specific spatial
characteristics of Philadelphia's new hall. As I spent a good deal of
time refamiliarizing myself with this splendid ensemble, I vividly
remembered many life-changing afternoons and evenings in my early
teens hearing the Orchestra at the Academy of Music. I eventually
decided to concentrate on exploring the unique qualities of the
Orchestra itself, employing a wide array of contrasts in dynamics and
sounds to embolden the ear to discover a landmark new space in what
I hope will be a vivid new musical experience.

Two visual elements have influenced *Color Wheel*. Color wheels are
tools used by artists and designers "that teach color relationships by
organizing colors in a circle so you can visualize how they relate to
each other." Most color wheels show primary colors and myriads of
related hues. I feel that this piece concentrates on the bolder contrasts
of basic primary colors. (I sometimes see colors when I compose, and
the qualities of certain chords do elicit specific sensations in me—for
example, I see A-major as bright yellow). I've also been fascinated
with Sufi whirling dervishes and their ecstatic spinning. This work
may have some ecstatic moments, but it is full of tension, continuous
energy, and drive.

Harmonically the piece explores a wide gamut of colors, from huge
overtone-derived chords, strongly contrasting levels of consonance
and dissonance, and occasional touches of jazz harmony and
syncopation (resurfacing from a period of study during high school
at the old Temple University Annex on Walnut Street).

Color Wheel opens with a brief, bold, chorale-like introduction that
introduces many of the piece's basic musical elements that will be
varied later on. These opening harmonies and vital 4- and 8-note
motifs in the horns and trumpets will reappear later in many guises.
The boldness of the opening chords is contrasted with the soft, liquid
harmonies and rising lines in the strings. *Color Wheel* then changes

character suddenly, beginning again with a contrastingly lighter tone as a scherzo in the winds. From then on, the work unfolds as a series of variations on the extremely malleable opening ideas. In fact, the work is a series of inventions on those initial harmonies and musical motifs.

After reaching a climactic point in its spinning, a variation of the slower music returns, passing rising melodic lines between sections of the strings. The faster music returns gradually in a series of more compressed variations and reexaminations of elements from before. The work builds to a whirling high point and closes with a return of the opening chorale idea in its grandest harmonic context and most fully realized melodic shape.

Color Wheel is dedicated with love to my wife, Evelyne Luest.

—Aaron Jay Kernis

ABOUT THE COMPOSER:

Aaron Jay Kernis is one of the youngest composers ever to be awarded the Pulitzer Prize in music (for his String Quartet No. 2 in 1998). He is among the most esteemed musical figures of his generation, with his compositions bearing the unmistakable stamp of a wildly fertile musical imagination forged out of the wide-ranging musical languages of the 1980s and '90s. His music bursts with rich poetic imagery, brilliant instrumental color, distinctive musical wit, and infectious exuberance.

PHOTO BY KIM PLUTI

Kernis has created and nurtured a distinctive personal voice. His work is as likely to be inspired by the horrors of the Persian Gulf War (as in the much-talked about Symphony No. 2) as the love poems of Anna Swir (*Love Scenes*); the earthy rhythms of Salsa (*100 Greatest Dance Hits*) or the antics of a child (*Before Sleep and Dreams*); the surrealism of Gertrude Stein (*Fragments of Gertrude Stein*) or the complexities and high craftsmanship of Italian mosaics (*Invisible Mosaic III*).

Kernis's music figures prominently on orchestral, chamber, and recital programs around the world. He has written works for many of classical music's foremost institutions and artists, including pieces premiered by Joshua Bell, Carter Brey, Renée Fleming, Pamela Frank, Julie Giacobassi, Sharon Isbin, Truls Mørk, and Nadja Salerno-Sonnenberg, as well as a monumental choral symphony, entitled *Garden of Light*, commissioned by the Disney Company to usher in the new millennium in 2000.

A Philadelphia native, Aaron Jay Kernis began musical studies on the violin. He began teaching himself piano at age 12 and started composing the following year. He continued studies at the San Francisco Conservatory of Music, Manhattan School of Music, and the Yale School of Music, working with composers as diverse as John Adams, Charles Wuorinen, and Jacob Druckman.

Kernis received national acclaim for his first orchestral work, *Dream of the Morning Sky*, premiered by the New York Philharmonic at the 1983 Horizons Festival. In addition to his 1998 Pulitzer Prize, his many awards have included the Stoeger Prize from the Chamber Music Society of Lincoln Center, a Guggenheim Fellowship, the Rome Prize, an NEA grant, a Bearns Prize, a New York Foundation for the Arts Award, and three BMI Student Composer Awards. He currently serves as the Minnesota Orchestra's New Music Advisor. Kernis's music is published by Associated Music Publishers.

TRIPLE CONCERTO IN C MAJOR, OP. 56 (FOR PIANO, VIOLIN, CELLO, AND ORCHESTRA)
composed 1803–1804 and given its public premiere in May 1808

Ludwig van Beethoven
born in Bonn on December 17, 1770
died in Vienna on March 26, 1827

This concerto runs about 35 minutes in performance. Beethoven scored it for an ensemble comprised of flute, 2 oboes, 2 clarinets, 2 bassoons, 2 horns, 2 trumpets, timpani, and strings, in addition to the three soloists (playing piano, violin, and cello).

Beethoven's "Triple Concerto" is a unique creation. It has no true siblings among the composer's other pieces, and even its "cousins" among the works of other great composers are not as obviously related as one might expect.

Three instrumental soloists working in tandem with an orchestral ensemble were not unprecedented. Many *concertante* works from the 17th and 18th centuries—by Bach, Vivaldi, Handel, Mozart, Haydn, and others—feature lesser and greater numbers of solo players. In many of these, the soloists play parts more prominent and recognizably different from the ensemble work going on around them. But when Beethoven sat down to write the Triple Concerto in 1803, he intended to clear a new path through the musical woods. And, he knew, he must make a safe journey home from the other side of the forest.

The Triple Concerto, beyond being a sterling work to showcase a trio of soloists along with some admirable orchestral writing, is not always held in high esteem. Musically, it is often considered among Beethoven's less-than-perfect works. Or, as a consolatory gesture to those who can't imagine actually criticizing Beethoven-the-God, it is said to be awfully darn good, if only we didn't have Beethoven's other, later—and clearly greater—concertos to compare it to. Largely in the same vein, the Triple is sometimes tossed in with a number of other "experimental" recipes—the *Choral Fantasy* and the *Grosse fuge* come to mind as similarly misunderstood trial balloons—which, in and of themselves, don't always sound as if they turned out quite right. On the bright side, such "half-baked" (but delicious) works led Beethoven on to greater and more beloved musical works.

Reality comprises all such criticism, along with a variety of more subtle observations, both musical and extra-curricular—along with the incontrovertible fact that the Triple Concerto is just plain fun, for both audience and performers alike. Any presentation of it is sure not only to attract ticket buyers (the name Beethoven continues to command gold at the box office) but also to inspire concertgoers onto their feet for a rousing round of applause. Beethoven, regardless of the stretching and experimentation he attempted in this concerto, never lost his impeccable sense of pacing and style, and his deft handling of the three soloists (singly, in pairs, and as a trio) is utterly expressive and masterful.

We don't know exactly why or when Beethoven decided to try writing a concerto for three instruments. He made some sketches for such a work in 1802, but apparently abandoned the effort when a specific performance opportunity disappeared. A triple concerto is mentioned the following year in a letter from Beethoven's brother Carl to publishers Breitkopf & Härtel, and the work appears to have been more or less complete by the summer of 1804. Beethoven was 34 years old at the time, with creation of the Triple Concerto coming on the heels of the form-shattering Third Symphony ("Eroica") and just before the equally revolutionary Fourth Piano Concerto.

Many have tried to connect the idea of a concerto for these particular three instruments (piano, violin, and cello) to one of Beethoven's most important patrons, Archduke Rudolph. The 15-year-old Archduke began piano lessons with Beethoven the same winter the concerto was written, and it is not unreasonable to surmise that such a precocious student might ask for a special concerto. Rudolph did have a private orchestra back at the palace, and the concerto's relatively easy piano part is within the capabilities of a well-practiced and moderately accomplished player. (While such a pianist can play the notes, the concerto nevertheless requires a great artist to make the music soar in conjunction with the two string soloists, an orchestra, and a collaborative conductor.) Nevertheless, there are no hard facts or surviving documentation supporting a major role for Rudolph in the concerto's creation. And, although Beethoven dedicated many later works to the Archduke, the inscription in the printed score of the Triple Concerto is to another patron, Prince Lobkowitz, in whose house a private first performance probably took place in 1804.

The opening movement of the Triple Concerto is expansive, both in sheer length and in atmosphere. The mere fact of having three soloists on stage accounts for some of this, and the time required to pass musical themes and countermelodies among them equally (although Beethoven seems to give the cellist extra moments of exposure and/or virtuosity). Alternating sections of activity and languorous repose carry us through several possible endings before Beethoven chooses to at last close the movement with a grand flourish.

Beethoven was a master of juxtaposition, and he follows the expansive first movement with a brief middle movement, whose enticing main theme, as played by the cello soloist, takes us directly into the third-movement finale. Here Beethoven takes inspiration from a gentle *polonaise* before swinging us head-over-heels into a brilliant allegro, gives us the faintest suggestion of a cadenza for all three instruments (almost as if they decide to play a minute of chamber music while the orchestra waits), and then ends the whole grand affair with an emphatically convincing flourish.

—Eric Sellen

SUITE NO. 2 FROM *DAPHNIS AND CHLOÉ*
from the ballet score composed 1909–12 and premiered on June 8, 1912

Maurice Ravel
born in Ciboure on March 7, 1875
died in Paris on December 28, 1937

This suite runs about 15 minutes in performance. Ravel scored it for a large ensemble comprised of piccolo, 2 flutes, alto flute, 2 oboes, English horn, 3 clarinets, bass clarinet, 3 bassoons, contrabassoon, 4 horns, 4 trumpets, 3 trombones, tuba, timpani, percussion (bass drum, field drum, snare drum, cymbals, triangle, tambourine, castanets, glockenspiel), 2 harps, celesta, and strings, plus an optional mixed chorus (singing without words).

The music for *Daphnis and Chloé* premiered in 1912 amidst an outpouring of new ballet scores commissioned by impresario Sergei Diaghilev. Diaghilev's Ballets Russes had swept into town in 1909, tingling and teasing Paris ballet audiences with freshly choreographed versions of Russian orchestral works such as Borodin's *Prince Igor* and Rimsky-Korsakov's *Scheherazade*. But Diaghilev wanted even fresher sounds for his dancing stageshows, and set about commissioning new music. In addition to Ravel's *Daphnis* in 1912, three epochal scores came from Igor Stravinsky: the dramatic *Firebird* in 1910, the mesmerizing *Petrushka* in 1911, and the cataclysmic *Rite of Spring* in 1913. At the time, Paris was as excitingly cutting-edge as any place in the world musically—and in other art forms as well (think of Henri Matisse and Pablo Picasso, just beginning their long years of creativity). In arts and letters, only Vienna rivaled the avant-garde excitement of the French capital.

Daphnis and Chloé predates many of Ravel's more popular orchestral works, including *La Valse, Boléro,* and the G-major and Lefthanded piano concertos. For a composer often satisfied (or obsessed) with focus and brevity, the complete *Daphnis and Chloé* is, in fact, Ravel's longest orchestral composition (running about 50 minutes). It is also perhaps the most masterful example of his consummate artistry as an orchestrator and colorist—of his ability to evoke a myriad of aural shadings from different instrumental groupings and playing techniques. As such, the score artfully displays the collaborative and individual virtuosity of any orchestra that performs it—and, quite appropriately for this evening's first concert by The Philadelphia Orchestra in its new home, offers a kaleidoscopic overview of a hall's potential as sonic "dance partner."

The story of the ballet's title characters is of Greek origin, transcribed by Longus, a writer who lived sometime between the second and fourth centuries A.D. It is a story of young love and the awakening of sexual desires. Set in rural antiquity, Daphnis and Chloé are youthful shepherd and shepherdess of uncertain parentage. Their burgeoning and lustful romance inspires the action through a series of adventures (dramatically helpful for staging as a ballet), including amorous rivalries, abductions, and other plot twists. Chance encounters and timely disclosures reveal that both hero and heroine are descended from aristocratic families, thus propelling the pair into a new life together with a grand and festive wedding. (The musical excerpts in Suite No. 2 portray only a few scenes from the full story.)

In 1909, Diaghilev asked Ravel to write music for his Ballet Russes company. Diaghilev's choreographer, Michel Fokine, sketched a storyline based on Longus's tale, and Ravel, after offering some suggested changes to the basic outline, began writing. The score's *Bacchanale* finale gave the composer some trouble, delaying its completion. Finally, in the winter of 1911–12, the work went into rehearsal, only to become the basis for ongoing tension and disagreement between Fokine and the company's star dancer, Vaslav Nijinsky, who was to portray Daphnis onstage. Diaghilev had to act as mediator among all the parties and even asked Ravel if they could forgo the wordless chorus in order to save money.

Somehow everything came together for the premiere in June 1912, with Pierre Monteux conducting. While critical and public reaction to the ballet on stage was considerably mixed, everyone seemed to love the musical score, from which Ravel soon extracted two different suites for performance without dancers. The second of these, corresponding roughly to the last of the ballet's three major scenes, soon gained enormous popularity in the concert hall and, along with Ravel's later orchestral works, helped establish the composer as one of the early 20th century's great musical figures.

The beginning of the ballet's final scene, which opens the Second Suite, depicts "Daybreak" after Daphnis's long night of despair and hopeless longing. In this exquisite music, Ravel magically portrays the sounds of nature just before the sun breaks above the horizon for a new day, while at the same time signaling the reawakening of hope in Daphnis's heart. The couple is fortuitously reunited and their future life together is foretold in pantomime. The closing *Bacchanale* brings forth general celebrating, seamlessly (if oddly) written in 5/4 time. The strange meter caused many rehearsal headaches and missteps for dancers in the original 1912 production, but also (almost magically) adds vibrancy and bounce to the music itself.

—Eric Sellen ■

THE PHILADELPHIA ORCHESTRA

A New Century, A New Home

On November 16, 1900, Fritz Scheel, a tall, imposing man sporting a handlebar mustache, ascended the podium to conduct the very first concert of The Philadelphia Orchestra in the city's beautiful Academy of Music.

One hundred years later to the day, on November 16, 2000, The Philadelphia Orchestra's current music director, Wolfgang Sawallisch, one of the most renowned conductors of our time, stood in the same spot to lead a gala concert celebrating a century of glorious music-making.

The party extended far beyond that one evening. Indeed, it went on for two years and touched more than one million lives. The Orchestra journeyed from its home stage to other parts of the city with a series of free "Neighborhood Concerts," and beyond—to the Carolinas and Florida, to Carnegie Hall, and to the music capitals of Europe and Asia.

In the same celebratory period, the Orchestra invited eight composers to write new Centennial Commissions (scheduling the works' premieres over four seasons, from 1998 to 2002), published a definitive history of the ensemble's first century, and issued a remarkable 12-CD retrospective of historic recordings and broadcasts. Spanning nine decades and encompassing 44 selections by 33 composers, with 17 conductors and 17 guest artists, the CD collection was culled from a massive library of recorded performances; many of the selections included had never before been commercially available.

In all, it was an anniversary year filled with triumphs for the 100-plus "Fabulous Philadelphians" (an affectionate sobriquet that caught on decades ago).

A NEW HOME
Just a year after the Centennial Celebration, The Philadelphia Orchestra reaches another milestone, one it has dreamed of for decades: playing in a new home especially created for it.

The Academy of Music, beloved though it is by all of Philadelphia—including The Philadelphia Orchestra—is an opera house, not a symphony hall. Verizon Hall at The Kimmel Center for the Performing Arts will expose Philadelphians for the first time to the full sonic splendor of the "Philadelphia Sound," recognized and admired from one end of the world to the other. That sound—rich and intense, with a sureness of intonation and phrasing, plus an enormous variety in shading and color—is as much a part of Philadelphia as the Museum of Art or the Declaration of Independence.

Ironically, until now, those who have been privileged to hear The Philadelphia Orchestra at its best were audience members in great halls *outside* Philadelphia: the Concertgebouw in Amsterdam, for instance, or Vienna's Musikverein, and, closer to home, Carnegie Hall in New York City. Now, The Kimmel Center's Verizon Hall joins that elite roster, an acoustic instrument designed specifically to complement the orchestra it houses.

Visually, too, audiences find something very different from the Academy in the elegantly cello-shaped Verizon Hall: not only unimpeded sight lines throughout the hall, but also a sense of intimacy, of being in the same space as their favorite musicians, communicating with them and sharing in the power and joy of music.

A CENTURY OF ACHIEVEMENT
A major factor in The Philadelphia Orchestra's continuing renown has been a continuity of leadership. There have been only six music directors during its first hundred years of music-making. Each has built solidly upon the past, knowing how precious that heritage is, while at the same time looking to the future and shaping the ensemble to his own special vision. Thus, the famous "Philadelphia Sound" has been created and nurtured into a special living legacy, revered throughout the world and unduplicated in any other city with any other group of musicians.

Technologically, The Philadelphia Orchestra has consistently been at the forefront, being the first to use the electrical method for commercial recording, to record on long-playing disks, to have its own sponsored national radio series, to perform on a movie soundtrack, and to appear on a national TV broadcast. In 1997, it was the first major American orchestra to present a live cybercast of a concert on the Internet.

Touring has been an important part of the Orchestra's activities from early on, spreading its fame and artistry across the globe. Out-of-town concerts began in the very first year, and regular appearances along the eastern seaboard soon followed. After World War I, the Orchestra

LEFT: THE PHILADELPHIA ORCHESTRA'S
CENTENNIAL TOUR OF EUROPE IN 2000.
[PHOTO BY JUDITH KURNICK]

BELOW, TOP: OVER THE PAST DECADE, THE
PHILADELPHIA ORCHESTRA HAS DEVELOPED A
SERIES OF POPULAR ANNUAL CONCERTS FOR A
VARIETY OF HOLIDAYS THROUGHOUT THE YEAR,
INCLUDING VALENTINE'S DAY, MARTIN LUTHER
KING DAY, AND HALLOWEEN, WHEN THE
ORCHESTRA'S MUSICIANS JOIN IN THE "SPIRIT" OF
FUN BY DONNING COSTUMES ALONG WITH THE
AUDIENCE. [PHOTO BY KELLY & MASSA]

BELOW, BOTTOM: MAESTRO WOLFGANG
SAWALLISCH ADDRESSES THE AUDIENCE DURING A
FAMILY CONCERT, WHICH FEATURED CHILDREN
AND GRANDCHILDREN OF PHILADELPHIA
ORCHESTRA MEMBERS IN A PERFORMANCE
OF LEOPOLD MOZART'S "TOY" SYMPHONY.
[PHOTO BY JEAN E. BRUBAKER]

FRITZ SCHEEL, A GERMAN-BORN MUSICIAN STEEPED IN THE ROMANTIC TRADITION, WAS THE PHILADELPHIA ORCHESTRA'S FIRST CONDUCTOR. [PHOTO COURTESY OF THE PHILADELPHIA ORCHESTRA ASSOCIATION ARCHIVES]

CARL POHLIG, WHO HAD ASSISTED GUSTAV MAHLER AT THE VIENNA STATE OPERA, TOOK OVER THE CONDUCTOR'S POST IN PHILADELPHIA AFTER THE DEATH OF FRITZ SCHEEL IN 1907. [PHOTO COURTESY OF THE PHILADELPHIA ORCHESTRA ASSOCIATION ARCHIVES]

LEOPOLD STOKOWSKI, THE LONDON-BORN CONDUCTOR WHO LED THE ORCHESTRA FOR NEARLY THREE DECADES FROM 1912 TO 1941, PUT PHILADELPHIA ON THE WORLD MUSICAL MAP. [PHOTO COURTESY OF THE PHILADELPHIA ORCHESTRA ASSOCIATION ARCHIVES]

THROUGH 44 YEARS AND NEARLY 400 RECORDINGS, EUGENE ORMANDY BUILT ON STOKOWSKI'S BASE TO MAKE THE PHILADELPHIA ORCHESTRA'S UNIQUE SOUND AND ARTISTRY RECOGNIZABLE THROUGHOUT THE WORLD. [PHOTO COURTESY OF THE PHILADELPHIA ORCHESTRA ASSOCIATION ARCHIVES]

RICCARDO MUTI BROUGHT A MAGNETIC PRESENCE AND INTENSE APPROACH TO MUSIC, AS WELL AS GREAT EXPERTISE IN CONDUCTING OPERA. [PHOTO © HENRY GROSSMAN, COURTESY OF THE PHILADELPHIA ORCHESTRA ASSOCIATION ARCHIVES]

A CONSUMMATE MUSICIAN WHOSE INTERPRETATIONS HAVE BECOME EVER MORE PROFOUND, WOLFGANG SAWALLISCH HAS BEEN AT THE HELM OF THE PHILADELPHIA ORCHESTRA SINCE 1993. [PHOTO BY CHRIS LEE]

moved westward to Chicago and St. Louis. In 1936, and again in 1937, the ensemble embarked upon an ambitious month-long transcontinental tour with Leopold Stokowski. The Philadelphians were the first orchestra to cross the Atlantic Ocean following World War II, and the first to play in the People's Republic of China and in Vietnam. In all, the Orchestra has made 25 tours beyond the shores of North America. Each season it embarks upon a major tour, either domestic or overseas, as well as a regular series of appearances at New York's Carnegie Hall, where the Philadelphians play more concerts each season than any other major American orchestra.

Performing the music of its own time, as well as of the past, has been part of the Orchestra's mission from the beginning. Its list of world premieres includes works by such composers as Barber, Bartók, Bolcolm, Copland, Del Tredici, Ginastera, Hanson, Hindemith, Rachmaninoff, Rands, Rouse, Varèse, and Webern. An ongoing commissioning program assures that the finest contemporary composers continue to join the list.

Philadelphia led the way in employing its musicians year-round, in hiring a woman for a full-time position other than the traditional role as harpist, and in forming a permanent volunteer group that would be active in fundraising and ancillary activities. And, from the beginning, it has considered paramount its responsibilities to the city in which it resides.

SERVING A HOMETOWN

The Philadelphia Orchestra emerged out of a series of concerts, conducted by Fritz Scheel, in the spring of 1900 to raise relief funds for widows and orphans of the Spanish-American War. From the success, both financial and artistic, of these concerts, a permanent annual orchestra was formed, with Scheel its first leader. Quickly the fledgling ensemble showed its mettle. The Orchestra invited Richard Strauss to conduct a program of his own music, presented the debut of the young Polish pianist Arthur Rubinstein, and initiated the now highly popular series of annual performances at Carnegie Hall.

Scheel was succeeded in 1907 by Carl Pohlig, former music director at the Stuttgart court and assistant to Gustav Mahler. Perhaps his greatest contribution was to invite the Russian composer-pianist Sergei Rachmaninoff to guest-conduct the Orchestra, thus beginning a long and close association.

In 1912 Pohlig was followed by the man who first brought The Philadelphia Orchestra international fame: Leopold Stokowski, a charismatic London-born musician and devotee of contemporary music, whose seminal works he introduced to a sometimes resistant public.

Adored by the young, Stokowski created an immensely popular youth series, which featured everything from llamas to a xylophone-playing motorcycle cop. He began a student competition whose winners would play with the Orchestra; now called the Albert M. Greenfield Competition, it has provided more than 400 brilliant young talents a first chance at professional performance. In an effort to assure the Orchestra a future roster of the finest musicians, Stokowski helped to found a conservatory, the renowned Curtis Institute of Music, whose graduates today make up roughly half of The Philadelphia Orchestra.

The Orchestra owes the initial development of its unique sound—as well as its entry into the recording field—to Stokowski. He collaborated with Walt Disney on one of the most popular films of all time, *Fantasia*, for which the Philadelphians performed the major part of the soundtrack.

Stokowski's handpicked successor was the Hungarian-born Eugene Ormandy, who remained at the helm for a remarkable 44 years. Ormandy was devoted both to the city and to the ensemble, and, in return, he was greatly admired by both. Building upon the unique sound created by Stokowski, Ormandy elicited an enviable richness and solidity of tone and virtuosity of execution from his players. He helped the Orchestra to amass one of the finest collections of stringed instruments in the world and brought in top players, many of them Americans. Possessed of an impeccable ear and an extraordinary memory for scores, Ormandy was especially at home in the Romantic repertoire, but he also conducted the American premieres of many important works. He took over the series of free open-air summer concerts that Stokowski had begun at the Robin Hood Dell in Fairmount Park (now held at the Mann Center for the Performing Arts), and he also established the Orchestra's nationally regarded summer residency at the Saratoga Performing Arts Center in upstate New York. Ormandy's catalogue of recordings, numbering nearly 400, includes three gold records and remains one of the largest and most acclaimed recorded legacies of any orchestra from the LP era.

In 1980, the Italian conductor Riccardo Muti took over as music director. A master of the core symphonic literature, Muti combined a magnetic stage presence with impeccable musicianship and scholarship, resulting in performances that were often electrifying. Refining the Orchestra's sound to fit the style of different composers and periods, he lent the ensemble a crisp, modern sheen. He introduced the Orchestra and the city to many older works that were largely unknown here, some of which became part of his discography with the Philadelphians. By inviting the esteemed composer Richard Wernick to become his advisor on contemporary music, Muti also assured the inclusion of significant new works in the ensemble's repertoire. Concerned about future audiences, he opened dress rehearsals to students.

A man of vast operatic experience, now director of Milan's La Scala, Muti initiated a tradition in Philadelphia of presenting concert versions of opera; these inspired international excitement and are still recalled with reverence by opera lovers. Muti typically spoke in the Academy Ballroom prior to these performances, illustrating his remarks elegantly at the piano. He was similarly devoted to chamber music, initiating a fine series of concerts featuring Philadelphia Orchestra musicians, now in its 17th season.

INTO A NEW CENTURY

Wolfgang Sawallisch became the sixth music director of The Philadelphia Orchestra in 1993, having had a distinguished two-decade career as head of the Bavarian State Opera in Munich.

Known around the world as one of the greatest exponents of the central European musical tradition, he is equally at home with contemporary music. It was thanks to Sawallisch that The Philadelphia Orchestra's centennial subscription series in 1999–2000 was devoted entirely to works composed during the ensemble's first 100 years. That decision was greeted with some skepticism, but it resulted in critical acclaim, box office success, and delighted audiences. Known as a fine pianist and chamber musician, Sawallisch also frequently performs in the Orchestra's chamber music series.

During Wolfgang Sawallisch's tenure, The Philadelphia Orchestra has taken an ever-increasing role in education and community enrichment. Pre-concert "Conversations" now enrich the audience's experience of every regular season concert. "Access Concerts," begun just last season, are drawing new audiences in through informal, inexpensive evenings with personable conductor-hosts. Young people, from pre-kindergarten through high school, enjoy special programs tailored to their age. Mindful that attending the Orchestra at normal prices can be prohibitive for some, the Orchestra continues its long-term commitment to providing low-cost tickets, offering specially priced Kimmel Center tickets on the day of each performance through its "Community Rush" and "Student Rush" programs.

A few years ago, when Wolfgang Sawallisch announced his intention to retire from The Philadelphia Orchestra's music directorship, he indicated that he would willingly stay on until his successor was found and in place. This generosity of spirit is typical of a man whose warmth and affection for the ensemble are palpable. Both musicians and audiences return that affection fully and marvel at this artist's superlative musicianship, which seems to deepen with each year. Maestro Sawallisch will not only open The Kimmel Center but, as Laureate Conductor, will be welcomed back each year for several weeks of concerts.

In January 2001 Christoph Eschenbach was named as The Philadelphia Orchestra's next music director; his tenure begins in 2003. Eschenbach is Conductor Laureate of the Houston Symphony Orchestra, which he brought into a position of eminence as music director, and he is at the helm of orchestras in Paris and Hamburg as well as the Ravinia Festival, summer home of the Chicago Symphony. A brilliant solo pianist and chamber musician, he has had a strong relationship with The Philadelphia Orchestra for three decades. Following his appointment as the new music director here, Eschenbach was described by the *Philadelphia Inquirer* as "a man of immense musical range and energy—and, more important, of serious, prodigious musical appetite." He makes his debut as music director-designate with The Philadelphia Orchestra with a week of concerts in February 2002, during The Kimmel Center's first season as the Orchestra's new home.

A SOUND FUTURE

The Kimmel Center is the fruition of a long-held dream for the citizens of Philadelphia and for the world-renowned Orchestra that proudly carries the city's name throughout the world. That the dream has become a reality is a testament to many extraordinarily gifted and generous people. The most instrumental of these individuals are acknowledged elsewhere in this book. But central to the process have been the tireless efforts of The Philadelphia Orchestra itself over the past two decades, represented artistically by its musicians and music director, and administratively by Joseph H. Kluger (president since 1989) and Richard L. Smoot (chair of the Board of Directors since the end of 2000).

As the Orchestra takes up residence in its new hall, it is mindful of its great responsibility to the City of Philadelphia and the larger world as the guardian of a musical tradition and an inspiration for future generations. With The Kimmel Center for the Performing Arts providing the setting that The Philadelphia Orchestra has so long desired, the true Philadelphia Sound will finally be revealed to audience members in all its glory. And this is as it should be, for as our city's "ambassador to the world," The Philadelphia Orchestra, in the end, belongs to the city, as does the marvelous building it calls home. ∎

ADMINISTRATIVE STAFF

of The Philadelphia Orchestra

JOSEPH H. KLUGER, PRESIDENT
SHELDON L. THOMPSON, EXECUTIVE VICE PRESIDENT
MIMI O'MALLEY, EXECUTIVE ASSISTANT TO THE PRESIDENT AND TO THE MUSIC DIRECTOR

ARTISTIC PLANNING AND OPERATIONS

SIMON WOODS, DIRECTOR

ARTISTIC PLANNING

ERICA FOX ZABUSKY,
ARTISTIC COORDINATOR

ALICIA LIN, ARTISTIC
ADMINISTRATION
ASSISTANT

MARCUS HALPER, DRIVER
AND ARTIST ASSISTANT

ORCHESTRA OPERATIONS

LIZ KINTZ,
OPERATIONS MANAGER

GEORGE BLOOD,
RECORDING ENGINEER

EDUCATION AND COMMUNITY PARTNERSHIPS

GARY ALAN WOOD,
DIRECTOR

AGNES FUNG,
PROJECT MANAGER

JENNY IMM,
EDUCATION
COORDINATOR

HYUNJIN PARK,
ADMINISTRATIVE ASSISTANT

EMPLOYEE RESOURCES

ELIZABETH WARSHAWER,
CHIEF PEOPLE OFFICER

HUMAN RESOURCES

SUSAN BANEY,
EMPLOYMENT MANAGER

KIMBERLY CAPONE,
BENEFITS SPECIALIST

DEANNA ARITAN,
OFFICE SERVICES
ADMINISTRATOR

ORCHESTRA MANAGEMENT

LOURDES STARR DEMERS,
PERSONNEL MANAGER

MARSHALL MENTZ,
ASSISTANT PERSONNEL
MANAGER

JEFFRY KIRSCHEN,
AUDITION COORDINATOR

ADMINISTRATION

INFORMATION TECHNOLOGY

LETITIA HURLEY, DIRECTOR

EZRA WIESNER,
SYSTEMS ANALYST I

WARREN KRYSIAK,
SYSTEMS ANALYST II

ARTHUR CURTIS,
DATABASE MANAGER

TIMOTHY LEE,
WEB COORDINATOR

ARCHIVES

JOANNE E. BARRY,
ARCHIVIST

DEVELOPMENT

JULIE DÍAZ, DIRECTOR

ELLEN-MARIE BONNER,
DEPUTY DIRECTOR

MATTHEW PRINCIPE,
ADMINISTRATIVE ASSISTANT

DEVELOPMENT OPERATIONS

REBECCA SMACKEY,
MANAGER OF
DEVELOPMENT
COMMUNICATIONS

ALICIA SALMONI, MANAGER
OF DEVELOPMENT SERVICES
AND RESEARCH

GINA RANGE, MANAGER
OF GIFT PROCESSING

NICOLE CARRAS,
DEVELOPMENT RESEARCH
COORDINATOR

SEAN LIPMAN,
GIFT PROCESSING
REPRESENTATIVE

CARLANA PAGE,
GIFT PROCESSING
REPRESENTATIVE

KATHLEEN TOOMEY,
DEVELOPMENT SERVICES
ASSISTANT

MAJOR GIFTS

SUSAN S. GOULD,
DIRECTOR

RICH QUINN, SENIOR
MAJOR GIFTS OFFICER

CHRISTINE HENDERSON
MICKLETZ, MANAGER OF
STEWARDSHIP AND
PLANNED GIVING

REBECCA BOLDEN,
COORDINATOR OF
MAJOR GIFTS

MELISSA LOHMANN,
COORDINATOR OF
STEWARDSHIP AND
PLANNED GIVING

ANNUAL FUND

JANINE S. SCAFF, DIRECTOR

SARAH FRIEDMAN,
MANAGER OF
TELEFUNDING AND DIRECT
MAIL

CORPORATE AND FOUNDATION RELATIONS

ALISON R. GROVE,
DIRECTOR

ERIK MICHAEL, ASSISTANT
DIRECTOR OF CORPORATE
RELATIONS

LARRY PASSMORE,
DEVELOPMENT OFFICER,
FOUNDATIONS

ALLEN PINKNEY, JR.,
CORPORATE DEVELOPMENT
ASSISTANT

ACADEMY OF MUSIC FUNDRAISING

LINDA C. SCRIBNER,
DIRECTOR

ANNETTE JEFFREY,
PROGRAM BOOK
COORDINATOR

LAURA ELLENBOGEN,
DEVELOPMENT ASSOCIATE

MARGARET SPENCER,
DEVELOPMENT ASSOCIATE

VOLUNTEER SERVICES

MIMI FLANAGAN,
DIRECTOR OF VOLUNTEER
PROGRAMS

PAULETTE MARCHESANI,
VOLUNTEER LIAISON

PATRICE HAYDEN,
DEVELOPMENT ASSOCIATE

MARKETING AND PATRON SERVICES

J. EDWARD CAMBRON,
DIRECTOR

MARIA TUMOLO-DANA,
AUDIENCE DEVELOPMENT
MANAGER

KIM GONZAGA,
PROJECT MANAGER

JANICE MAKOWSKI,
ART DIRECTOR

LISA BRITTINGHAM-
DUHART, MARKETING
COORDINATOR

ALISON KREIGER,
JUNIOR GRAPHIC
DESIGNER

KARL U. BUCUS,
GROUP SALES ASSOCIATE

KATIE McGARVEY,
ASSISTANT TO THE
AUDIENCE DEVELOPMENT
MANAGER

PUBLIC RELATIONS

JUDITH KURNICK,
DIRECTOR

KATHERINE BLODGETT,
ASSISTANT DIRECTOR

EMMA SPONAUGLE,
PUBLIC RELATIONS
COORDINATOR

ERIC SELLEN,
PUBLICATIONS MANAGER

DARRIN T. BRITTING,
PROGRAM EDITOR

FINANCE

BENJAMIN HAYLLAR,
CHIEF FINANCIAL OFFICER

ADARE MCMILLAN,
CONTROLLER

TIM COOPER,
BUSINESS ANALYST/
PAYROLL SUPERVISOR

MARY KENNEDY-BART,
BUDGET ANALYST

JULIA DRISCOLL MORGAN,
ACCOUNTING ANALYST

ROXANNE J. VAILLETTE,
PAYROLL ADMINISTRATOR

GREG HORN, ACCOUNTING
ADMINISTRATOR

ADMINISTRATIVE OFFICES

THE ATLANTIC BUILDING
260 SOUTH BROAD STREET,
16TH FLOOR
PHILADELPHIA, PA 19102
PHONE: 215.893.1900
WWW.PHILORCH.ORG

TICKET OFFICE

TICKET PHILADELPHIA
THE KIMMEL CENTER
BROAD & SPRUCE STREETS
PHILADELPHIA, PA 19102
TICKETS: 215.893.1999

LEFT AND BELOW, TOP: BEGUN AS PART OF THE ORCHESTRA'S WORLDWIDE CENTENNIAL CELEBRATIONS IN 2000, ANNUAL "NEIGHBORHOOD CONCERTS" NOW FEATURE THE ENSEMBLE PERFORMING IN VARIOUS PARTS OF THE CITY, INCLUDING WEST PHILADELPHIA'S CLARK PARK (JULY 2001, BELOW) AND CENTER CITY'S RITTENHOUSE SQUARE (JUNE 2000, LEFT). [PHOTOS: CLARK PARK BY EMMA SPONAUGLE; RITTENHOUSE SQUARE BY COY BUTLER]

BELOW, BOTTOM: CHRISTOPH ESCHENBACH ANSWERS QUESTIONS AT THE NEWS CONFERENCE ON JANUARY 29TH ANNOUNCING HIM AS THE NEXT MUSIC DIRECTOR OF THE PHILADELPHIA ORCHESTRA. ESCHENBACH IS JOINED ON THE PLATFORM BY ORCHESTRA PRESIDENT JOSEPH H. KLUGER (CENTER) AND CHAIR RICHARD L. SMOOT (RIGHT). [PHOTO BY DON TRACY]

RESIDENT COMPANIES
OF THE KIMMEL CENTER AND THE ACADEMY OF MUSIC

THE OPERA COMPANY OF PHILADELPHIA

*G*rand opera is undergoing a renaissance in Philadelphia. Coinciding with the opening of The Kimmel Center is an equally momentous celebration for the Opera Company of Philadelphia: the beginning of a new era at its beautiful home, the Academy of Music.

To see that opera has come of age in Philadelphia, look no further than the first festive performances of this new era, which bring Denyce Graves to the Academy of Music. Graves has had a special relationship with Philadelphia audiences since her 1992 Opera Company debut as Carmen. In demand around the world, she demonstrates her loyalty to this city's opera lovers by offering them her much-anticipated title role debut in Offenbach's *La Périchole*.

The Opera Company, now entering its 26th year, plans its seasons around the central operatic repertoire of Italian, French, and German works, interspersed with lesser-known gems. This season, for example, opened with Donizetti's *Elixir of Love*, and, following *La Périchole* in January, includes Puccini's *Madama Butterfly*, Mozart's *Don Giovanni*, and Bellini's rarely performed but richly melodic *The Capulets and the Montagues*.

Producing Artistic Director Robert B. Driver's philosophy of casting promising young singers on their way to stardom pays off both in fine performances and in loyalty to the company. Such singers as sopranos

Left and next page: Scenes from the Opera Company's 2000 production of *The Magic Flute*, directed by Producing Artistic Director Robert B. Driver, who put a twist on Mozart's classic by setting it in an alluring rain forest.

Above: Baritone Gregg Baker, shown here making his role debut as Scarpia in the Opera Company's *Tosca*, is a Philadelphia favorite whom audiences have grown to love.

[Photos by Katharine Elliott]

Christine Brandes and Maureen O'Flynn, mezzo-soprano Stephanie Blythe, tenor William Burden, baritone Gregg Baker, and bass-baritone Arthur Woodley have become audience favorites over the years.

Created in 1975 from the merger of the Lyric and Grand Opera companies, the Opera Company has grown tremendously since Driver took leadership in 1991. Annual performances have increased from eight to 35, and subscriptions have jumped from 3,200 to more than 12,000, placing the Opera Company in the top tier of American companies. The opening of The Kimmel Center gives the Opera Company increased scheduling freedom at the Academy, as well as opportunities to produce innovative new works in Perelman Theater.

The Opera Company nurtures its ties with fine young singers studying at the Curtis Institute of Music and the Academy of Vocal Arts, often casting them in supporting roles. As part of their training, Curtis students are assigned "intern" roles in one opera each season, culminating in their singing at a special *sitzprobe*, or "seated rehearsal." Curtis graduates such as Rinat Shaham, Juan Diego Flórez, and Eric Owens have gone on to leading roles with the Company.

The Sounds of Learning™, an education program established in 1991 to introduce young people to opera, now involves 24 schools in Philadelphia and New Jersey. With curriculum provided by the Company's education staff, students study each opera in school and then attend the dress rehearsal, free of charge. Opera America, the profession's service organization, has called this the best opera education program in the nation.

In 1993, the Opera Company opened its own production facility in Northeast Philadelphia, which has attracted some of the nation's best creative teams. Their original productions are rented out, earning money for the Company. Acclaimed Polish artist Rafal Olbinski will make his U.S. design debut by creating the Company's production of *Don Giovanni* this March.

The Principal Conductor of the Opera Company, Maurizio Barbacini, debuted with the Company in 1994 and has been on staff since 1998. Maestro Barbacini brings with him a deep knowledge of classic Italian and French repertoire and has become a key member of the artistic staff.

Also vital to the Opera Company's success is Executive Director Jack Mulroney. Following 15 years of board leadership, during which he is credited with steering the Company through difficult financial waters, Mulroney joined the staff in 1998.

The 2000–2001 season brought the Opera Company of Philadelphia great acclaim worldwide. A new production of Rossini's *Italian Girl in Algiers*, starring Stephanie Blythe and Juan Diego Flórez, was telecast live on WHYY-TV and broadcast on PBS in several national markets. The season finale, Gershwin's *Porgy and Bess*, starring Arthur Woodley and Kishna Davis, was the highest-selling opera in the Company's history.

The current season promises to continue the tradition of the finest of grand opera at the Academy of Music—America's opera house. ■

Mezzo-soprano Denyce Graves, pictured in her signature role of Carmen, gives Philadelphia another role debut in January with *La Périchole*. [Photo courtesy of Lyric Opera of Chicago]

OPERA COMPANY OF PHILADELPHIA
BOARD OF DIRECTORS

John P. Mulroney, Executive Director (left) and Robert B. Driver, Producing Artistic Director. [Photo by Nick Kelsh]

Officers

James B. Straw, President	Jack R. Bershad, Vice President	Laren Pitcairn, Vice President
C. Christopher Cannon, Chair	Richard A. Doran, Vice President	Roberto Sella, Vice President
Alan B. Miller, Chair Emeritus	Robert B. Driver, Vice President and Producing Artistic Director	Kenneth R. Swimm, Vice President
Dennis Alter, Vice Chair		Albert E. Piscopo, Vice President and Treasurer
Sara A. Cerato, Vice Chair	John P. Mulroney, Vice President and Executive Director	Rhea Mandell, Vice President and Secretary
Laurie Wagman, Vice Chair	Clifford E. Haines, Vice President	Gary H. Gansky, Associate Treasurer and Chief Financial Officer
Benjamin Alexander, Vice President	G. Thompson Pew, Jr., Vice President	

Board Members

Benjamin Alexander	Clifford E. Haines	Daria Pew
Dennis Alter	Richard J. Henry	G. Thompson Pew, Jr.
Ralph Amado	Carol Lawrence*	John W. Piasecki
Cynthia Archer	Lynne Lechter*	Albert E. Piscopo
Alice W. Beck	Gabriele Lee	Laren Pitcairn
Jack Bershad	Helen Lord	Bonnie R. Plunkett
Lisa B. Binder	Stephen Madva	Bernard J. Poussot
Elizabeth M. Bowden	Rhea Mandell	Marianne C. Raphaely
C. Christopher Cannon	Harriet E. G. Margolis	John D. Rollins
Sara A. Cerato	Mario Mele	Lionel Savadove
Georgette Ciukurescu	Alan B. Miller	Roberto Sella
Betsy Z. Cohen	John P. Mulroney	Karl H. Spaeth
Colin S. Diver	Donald P. Mykytiuk	James B. Straw
Richard A. Doran	Richard G. Nadeau	Kenneth R. Swimm
Frank Giordano	Brian J. O'Neill*	Pina Templeton
Rosalie Burns Goldberg	Constantine Papadakis	Anna C. Verna*
	Ruth E. Perry	Laurie Wagman

*Ex officio

PENNSYLVANIA BALLET

When Pennsylvania Ballet staged its first production of *The Taming of the Shrew* during its Spring 2001 season, audiences couldn't believe what they were seeing. The leading lady, Katharina, smashed a lute over the head of her sister's suitor, fell off a horse, and slapped her lover's face so loudly you could hear it in the back rows of the Academy of Music.

In the hands of a less gifted company, the goings-on might have come across as slapstick. But the elegant and versatile Pennsylvania Ballet managed to retain the delicacy—as well as the farce—of Shakespeare's story, whose inventive choreography was by another Englishman, the late John Cranko.

Since its 1963 debut, Pennsylvania Ballet has performed more than 200 different ballets, including a diverse classical repertoire and an impressive number of commissioned works. At the heart of its offerings are more than 30 works by the Russian-born choreographer George Balanchine, including such favorites as *Serenade*, *A Midsummer Night's Dream*, and *The Nutcracker*, which is presented every holiday season. Indeed, so closely linked is the company with Balanchine that when a Balanchine Celebration was held at the Kennedy Center in Washington, D.C., in 2000, Pennsylvania Ballet was invited to perform, along with a handful of other companies, including the legendary Bolshoi.

From the beginning, Pennsylvania Ballet dancers have demonstrated technical mastery, versatility, and exuberance. These qualities are very much in evidence today, as witnessed in a *New York Times* review from February 2001: "Another of the afternoon's pleasures was the performers' crisp, musical and beautifully schooled classicism and infectious delight in dancing." The dancers, now numbering 40, show loyalty to the company, often remaining throughout their careers. A seamless ensemble, they can move from the perfect corps discipline required by some ballets to the star turns beloved by audiences.

Pennsylvania Ballet grew out of a ballet school formed by Barbara Weisberger, a Balanchine protégé. Weisberger's energy and vision helped move the company quickly to the forefront of the regional ballet movement. In 1968, the company performed at City Center in New York City, gaining national credibility that led to a decade of touring and an appearance on the PBS series *Dance in America*.

Since 1994, Pennsylvania Ballet's Artistic Director has been Roy Kaiser, who rose through the ranks from the corps de ballet to Principal Dancer, then Ballet Master; under the company's former leader, Christopher d'Amboise, Kaiser served as Associate Artistic Director. Other contributors to the company's artistic vision include Ballet Mistresses Tamara Hadley and Sandra Jennings and Ballet Master Jeffrey Gribler, who retired from the stage in 2001 after 26 years with the company.

During Kaiser's tenure, Pennsylvania Ballet has premiered an array of classical and contemporary ballets for Philadelphia audiences, including David Parsons's *Mood Swing*, Agnes de Mille's *Rodeo*, Lar Lubovitch's *Waiting for the Sunrise*, George Balanchine's *Slaughter on Tenth Avenue*, Alvin Ailey's *The River*, Matthew Neenan's *Vicissitudes*, Paul Taylor's *Company B*, and a new staging of *Sleeping Beauty*. The company has also commissioned ballets from a diverse cross-section of choreographers, including Merce Cunningham, Kevin O'Day, Dwight Rhoden, David Parsons, Lynne Taylor-Corbett, and Val Caniparoli.

Pennsylvania Ballet has its own orchestra, with players drawn largely from the Philadelphia area. Their versatility matches that of the dancers: from the baroque precision of Bach to the romanticism of Alexander Glazunov, from the Englishman Henry Purcell to the American Morton Gould.

Under the leadership of Executive Director Michael G. Scolamiero, who joined the organization in 1997, the Pennsylvania Ballet has increased its subscriber base to more than 10,000. The company also attracts younger audiences, ages 18 to 32, through a series called "Thursday Night Jumps." One evening with characters such as the ballet prince in *Plush*, Trey McIntyre's inventive romp, ought to keep these audiences coming back. How many ballet princes have *you* seen lately dressed in fur and sporting spiky red hair? ∎

AMERICAN THEATER ARTS FOR YOUTH

*I*magine what it's like to be a student learning about the challenges and hopes of immigrants at Ellis Island through the medium of music theater. That is precisely what took place throughout the United States last year, thanks to the nation's leading presenter of professional, curriculum-related music theater for young audiences, American Theater Arts for Youth (TAFY). Through an original, high-spirited musical, *Ellis Island: Gateway to a Dream*, students encounter fictional characters from various ethnic backgrounds as they arrive on Ellis Island, facing new realities and holding onto old dreams.

"I really enjoyed the play!" wrote one fifth-grader. "I could just feel how much they wanted to get off that boat and into America. It really surprised me that the man from Poland believed that the streets were paved with gold and silver." Another student wrote that, having seen the play, she wanted to go to Ellis Island to find out whether her grandfather's name is engraved on the Wall of Honor.

Philadelphia-based American TAFY was founded in 1970 by Laurie Wagman, Chair, who continues to mold and guide the mission of the company. In the belief that theater arts can promote multiculturalism and foster teamwork, critical thinking, and creativity among young people, Wagman has strived to place theater at the center of school curricula. In addition to its performances, American TAFY works with many schools, offering study guides, workshops, residencies, and collaborative

Opposite page: *Beauty and the Beast*.
[© American TAFY]

Left: Scenic Designer Michael Triolo adds
the finishing touches to a toy soldier for
American TAFY's production of *Babes in
Toyland*. [Photo by Harvey Finkle]

Above, top: Founder and Chair Laurie
Wagman, Line Producer Don Kersey, and
Technical Director Jamey Jennings review
designs for an upcoming American TAFY
production. [Photo by Harvey Finkle]

Above, middle: *Alice in Wonderland*.
[© American TAFY]

Left: Costume Designer Tina Heinz with an actress being fitted for *Beauty and the Beast*. [Photo by Harvey Finkle]

Top right: *Babes in Toyland*. [© American TAFY]

Bottom right: Costumer Gretchen Ellis. [Photo by Harvey Finkle]

programs. These efforts further students' learning and help develop future audiences for the arts.

American TAFY performs its shows in major arts facilities nation-wide, reaching more than 1.4 million children annually. Each year, audiences in more than 400 cities regularly enjoy its original musicals on a regular basis. In 2001, TAFY produced, rehearsed, and mounted 26 tours, using the talents of more than 300 gifted professional actors, playwrights, composers, directors, costume designers, and technical personnel. Ms. Wagman calls their skills the "grit behind the glitter."

In addition, through its Reach for the Stars program, American TAFY hosts thousands of special-needs children each year, free of charge. Cast members, who meet and greet audiences after every performance, frequently make appearances at hospitals for children. The company also offers weekend performances for families, scouts, and a multifaceted range of community groups.

American TAFY's broad repertoire includes new musical adaptations of timeless works of fiction, including *Beauty and the Beast*, *Alice in Wonderland*, *A Christmas Carol*, *Tom Sawyer*, *Pinocchio*, and *Cinderella*. Other productions celebrate the diversity of the American experience (*Black Journey*, *Pied Piper of Harlem*, *Remember Angel*, etc.) and heroes in American history (*Ben Franklin*, *Abraham Lincoln*, *We the People*, etc.).

Some subjects are simply too emotionally laden for adequate treatment in history textbooks. One such subject is Anne Frank, the Dutch teenager who died in a concentration camp during World War II, but whose diary lives on as her legacy. American TAFY brought her story to life on the stage in 1996, and since then the company has performed its inspiring and poignant musical *Anne Frank—A Voice Heard* to well over 600,000 students and educators around the nation. Woven into the school curriculum, these performances prompted an outpouring of pictures, videos, and many thousands of letters from students addressed "Dear Anne."

American TAFY has received many awards, including one from the American Society of Educators, which named it the leading producer of theater for young audiences in the nation. Theater critics applaud its productions as well. "Again and again, American Theater Arts for Youth, Inc. proves how strong it is in creating original contemporary theater," commented the *New York Times*. Perhaps the spirit of American TAFY is best summed up by *Critics' Choice* magazine, which referred to the company as "a national cultural adventure."

"Despite its substantial growth," notes Wagman, "American Theater Arts for Youth continues to nurture the same close relationships with our hometown audiences that we did 30 years ago." As a Resident Company of The Kimmel Center's Perelman Theater, American TAFY looks forward to an exciting future of Philadelphia performances, including six favorite musicals in the opening season. ■

AMERICAN THEATER ARTS FOR YOUTH PRODUCTION COUNCIL

LAURIE WAGMAN,
FOUNDER/CHAIR.
[PHOTO BY HARVEY FINKLE]

ARTISTIC OPERATIONS

ROBERT STECK, DIRECTOR

DON KERSEY,
LINE PRODUCER

FLOYD BUSSIE

GRETCHEN ELLIS

LEE EVANS

TINA HEINZ

JAMEY JENNINGS

MARK KNOX

ROBERT MORGAN

SHANE MORTON

JEANNIE STITH

MICHAEL TRIOLO

JIM WADE

ADMINISTRATION/ EDUCATIONAL SERVICES

JOAN KNEPPER, DIRECTOR

ARNITA CLAITT

JEAN COVELLO

CARL DIPILLA

JODY HAGGERTY

ROSE NERI

JUDY OSTERNECK

TAMI RIGSBY

ALEX RILLING

JOANNA SPIOTTO

CLARENCE TUCKER

TANYA VLADIMIRSKY

AMY WOZNIAK

PLUS THE MORE THAN 300 DEDICATED PROFESSIONALS— PERFORMERS, DIRECTORS, CHOREOGRAPHERS, AUTHORS, COMPOSERS, ORCHESTRATORS, DESIGNERS, AND MORE— WHO BRING THEIR FINE TALENTS AND SKILLS TO AMERICAN TAFY PRODUCTIONS EACH YEAR.

THE CHAMBER ORCHESTRA OF PHILADELPHIA

It is not often that musical programming fits an occasion to perfection. But such is the case with the work that The Chamber Orchestra of Philadelphia has chosen to inaugurate its series at The Kimmel Center: a stunning multimedia production of Joseph Haydn's great oratorio *The Creation*, itself a kind of musical painting. Its subject, no less than the universe "in the beginning," will celebrate The Kimmel Center's "creation" as well.

Marc Mostovoy, the founder and artistic director of The Chamber Orchestra of Philadelphia (formerly known as Concerto Soloists), has long been in the forefront of successful efforts to marry classical music to the fine arts, using video projections and English supertitles. Using hundreds of images of great art from Renaissance to contemporary, Mostovoy's visual multimedia concept of the Haydn oratorio will take the viewer from chaos to creation, heaven to earth, darkness to light. Bringing the music vividly to life for the listener, Principal Conductor Ignat Solzhenitsyn will lead renowned vocal soloists, The Philadelphia Singers, and, of course, The Chamber Orchestra of Philadelphia.

Founded in 1964, Mostovoy's ensemble was born as Concerto Soloists Sixteen. The flexible group of fine local players was trained largely at Philadelphia's Curtis Institute of Music. Members of the ensemble were featured as soloists in concertos, then stepped back into the ensemble to accompany their colleagues. Smaller than a symphony orchestra, but

THE CHAMBER ORCHESTRA OF PHILADELPHIA IN
REHEARSAL AT THE ACADEMY OF VOCAL ARTS,
JULY 2001. [PHOTOS BY NICK KELSH]

significantly larger than a chamber music ensemble, Concerto Soloists excelled at intimate baroque and classical works of the 18th century as well as unusual pieces from the 19th and 20th centuries. Typically, the players stood rather than being seated. They performed with and without a conductor, depending on the repertoire and venue.

Concerto Soloists began to establish its reputation, touring and earning rave reviews in the United States, western and eastern Europe, and Israel. The *New York Times* applauded the ensemble for its "wonderful control, admirable enthusiasm...[and] sure sense of style," calling it "the most impressive small ensemble to come through Carnegie Hall in quite some time."

At home, Concerto Soloists became known as the city's "resident chamber orchestra." Its long-standing associations with the Academy of Vocal Arts, the Philadelphia Singers, the Mendelssohn Club, the Choral Arts Society, Singing City, the Opera Festival of New Jersey, the Sylvan Opera Company and others provide these performing arts organizations with a single, highly professional orchestra. And the ensemble continues to foster Mostovoy's multimedia treatment of masterworks, with such oratorios as Handel's *Israel in Egypt*, Bach's *St. John Passion*, and Vivaldi's popular *Four Seasons*.

The change in moniker to The Chamber Orchestra of Philadelphia recognizes a shift in artistic direction propelled by the gifted young Russian-born and Curtis-trained Ignat Solzhenitsyn. Bringing new

blood to the ensemble, Solzhenitsyn joined the Orchestra in 1993 as its Assistant Conductor, was soon elevated to the post of Associate Conductor, and was named Principal Conductor in 1998. Under his guidance, the Orchestra expanded its size so that it could regularly present larger works and perform a wider range of repertoire. Residency in the world-class Kimmel Center now enables the Orchestra to present a greater number of internationally acclaimed soloists and guest conductors. Solzhenitsyn, who is also renowned as a concert pianist, has performed as soloist with many of the world's most prestigious orchestras. He was recently described by the *Washington Post* as "an interpreter of probing intellect as well as an avid risk-taker."

The Chamber Orchestra of Philadelphia has doubled its number of performances for this season and is bringing in such high-profile guest soloists as cellists Mstislav Rostropovich and Steven Isserlis, soprano Sylvia McNair, pianists Gary Graffman and Susan Starr, violinist Cho-Liang Lin, the Romeros Guitar Quartet, and the chamber orchestra I Musici, as well as the popular violinist Mark O'Connor with the Metamorphosen Chamber Orchestra.

The *Philadelphia Inquirer* recently stated that The Chamber Orchestra "set an admirably high standard for future concerts ... this standard will also serve notice and provide inspiration to any other classical musicians in town." Thus, it is widely recognized that, now in its 37th year, the Orchestra is playing at the highest artistic level. ■

OPPOSITE PAGE: PHOTO BY NICK KELSH

CHAMBER ORCHESTRA OF PHILADELPHIA
BOARD OF DIRECTORS

JUDITH DOOLING,
EXECUTIVE DIRECTOR,
AND MARC MOSTOVOY,
ARTISTIC DIRECTOR, IN
PERELMAN THEATER,
SEPTEMBER 2001.
[PHOTO BY NICK KELSH]

KENNETH M. JARIN, CO-CHAIR

THOMAS J. KNOX, CO-CHAIR

WILLIAM H. ROBERTS, PRESIDENT

JOAN PARKER, VICE PRESIDENT

HARVEY G. MAGARICK, TREASURER

ROBERT DEE, SECRETARY

MARC S. MOSTOVOY, FOUNDER AND ARTISTIC DIRECTOR

JACINTO L. AYALA	G. MICHAEL MAIN
D. WALTER COHEN	LOUISE MCCABE
LEA MORRISON COHN	MARSHALL W. MEYER
LISA DETWILER	BERNADINE J. MUNLEY
W. MITCHELL FENIMORE, III	DONALD L. MYERS
CHARLES GOTTESMAN	MELBA PEARLSTEIN
LARRY GROSS	SUZANNE J. PECK
EDGAR HAMMERSHAIMB	LESTER P. SCHAEVITZ
BERNARD HEINZEN	NELSON SHANKS
JONATHAN HOFFMAN	KELLY BOYD SYLVESTER
LINDA KNOX	A. WESLEY WYATT
REAVES C. LUKENS, JR.	

PHILADANCO

*T*he Philadelphia Dance Company, known affectionately as
PHILADANCO, has been garnering praise for more than three decades
and continues to bring its unique blend of classical ballet, modern dance,
jazz, and African-American inspirations to audiences worldwide.

PHILADANCO was born 31 years ago, thanks to the determination of
Joan Myers Brown, who as its Executive Director continues to provide
the company's artistic vision. A Philadelphia native trained in ballet and
modern dance, Brown performed on Broadway and in top nightclubs with
the greats, including Pearl Bailey, Sammy Davis, Jr., and Cab Calloway.
But her dream was to open the world of concert dance to African
Americans, who had long been denied opportunities to perform with
major companies. Brown created the Philadelphia School of Dance,
which provided low-cost, high-quality training to area students, and
soon made up the nucleus for a new company.

At first, male dancers were scarce, but Brown recruited some football
players from a local high school, many of whom stayed with the company.
The troupe continued to grow, and its ranks soon included dancers
from around the world, including the Caribbean, Germany, the
Philippines, and Ethiopia.

Over the years, the company became known for its broad repertoire and diverse styles, and for the skill and dedication of its dancers. The repertoire, which often portrays aspects of the experiences and traditions of African Americans, has been developed by some of the most prominent choreographers in the nation, including Milton Myers (resident choreographer), Donald Byrd, Jawole Willa Jo Zollar, Blondell Cummings, Ron K. Brown, and Talley Beatty. PHILADANCO's programs are eclectic and have broad appeal. Original scores feature electronic and neo-classical music, modern jazz, and works by African composers, including Mali native Oumou Sangare, Africa's top recording artist, and the Nigerian singer, dancer, and composer Wunmi Olaiya.

PHILADANCO is now acknowledged as one of the top predominately African-American companies in the nation, along with the Alvin Ailey American Dance Theater and the Dance Theater of Harlem. An intense, 40-week-per-year touring schedule takes the troupe to cities throughout the U.S., Europe, and Asia. The company has performed with The Philadelphia Orchestra and the Duke Ellington Orchestra, and in premier venues like the Kennedy Center and Madison Square Garden. A recent TV appearance featured *The Xmas Files*, choreographed by Danny Ezralow, which aired on WHYY-TV as part of the series *Philadelphia Performs!*

PHILADANCO was among the first dance companies to offer its dancers full yearly contracts and to provide housing. Its success has spawned the desire to broaden awareness and opportunities for others. Both at home and on tour, the company provides lectures, workshops, and master classes and also performs in schools and community centers. PHILADANCO achieved worldwide recognition when it founded the International Conference for Black Dance Companies, first held in Philadelphia in 1988 with more than 80 in attendance. In 2001, 700 people attended the conference.

Throughout PHILADANCO's history, founder Joan Myers Brown has remained the company's guiding light, working 15 hours a day, seven days a week, at the West Philadelphia headquarters of her company and school—located, appropriately, on Philadanco Way. On the walls are enough plaques to fill a museum, but perhaps her most treasured is one that names her a "living legend" among women in dance.

The company Brown created is far more than a tribute to technical skill and interpretive know-how. In the words of *Dance Magazine*, the uniqueness of PHILADANCO is its ability to "represent the possibilities of the human spirit through dance." ■

PHOTO BY LOIS GREENFIELD

PHILADANCO
BOARD OF DIRECTORS

JOAN MYERS BROWN,
EXECUTIVE DIRECTOR
[PHOTO BY
DEBORAH BOARDMAN]

OFFICERS

SPENCER WERTHEIMER, CHAIR

H. HETHERINGTON SMITH, PRESIDENT

THOMAS L. LUSSENHOP, VICE PRESIDENT, ADMINISTRATION

HERBERT F. REID, JR., VICE PRESIDENT, FINANCE

J. ST. GIRARD JORDAN, SECRETARY

WILLIAM A. SMITH, PAST PRESIDENT

BOARD MEMBERS

BRIAN G. BAGNALL	JONATHAN W. MITCHELL
SCOTT BOOTH	ANTHONY K. MOORE
BARBARA KATZ CHOBERT	JERI PACKMAN
WILLIAM CHARLES DIXON	EVELYN R. SAMPLE
JEROME M. GIBBS	DONALD U. SMITH
CHARLES GREENE	HON. CAROLYN E. TEMIN
BEVERLY HARPER	IRENE Y. WAITZMAN
ALAN R. KUTNER	

BUSINESS ON BOARD'S PROGRAM OBSERVER

ALLISON FRANCIS

THE PHILADELPHIA CHAMBER MUSIC SOCIETY

*C*hamber music—works written for various types of small ensembles, with one instrument to a part—has many devout admirers among classical music lovers. Those who gravitate to this intimate form find that it reveals some of the most profound musical thoughts of the greatest composers.

Despite sporadic efforts over the years by chamber music devotees, Philadelphia did not really take hold as a destination for major ensembles until the Philadelphia Chamber Music Society (PCMS) came into being, under the devoted and skillful direction of Anthony P. Checchia, a bassoonist and music administrator. The Society grew out of a small series Checchia initiated in the late 1960s that featured ensembles from the renowned Marlboro Music School and Festival in Vermont (which Checchia has managed since 1959), supplemented by noted soloists.

The Philadelphia Chamber Music Society was incorporated in 1986, and its initial season was a sold-out success. From seven concerts the annual series soon jumped to 21, and it has continued to expand ever since, attracting virtually every eminent chamber ensemble in the world, as well as many of today's leading instrumental and vocal recitalists. For the 2001–2002 season, 55 concerts are scheduled, with all tickets sold at a modest price. The Philadelphia Chamber Music Society now presents the largest, most important series of its kind in the U.S. Since 1986, PCMS has been managed by Checchia and by noted composer Philip Maneval, who is Executive Director.

Opposite page: The Beaux Arts Trio.
[Photo by Christian Steiner]

Left: András Schiff.
[Photo by Thomas Miller]

Above: The Tokyo String Quartet.
[Photo by Christian Steiner]

By the close of the 2000–2001 season, the Society had hosted 42 recognized string quartets, ranging alphabetically from the Alban Berg to the Ying. In terms of frequency of performance, the world-renowned Guarneri String Quartet holds the record, with 17 appearances, followed by the Juilliard String Quartet at 15, and the Tokyo String Quartet at 14. A moving event last season was the final appearance of David Soyer as Guarneri cellist, with the bow being passed, so to speak, after 36 years, to Peter Wiley.

Also highly popular are various trios, notably the Beaux Arts, which has set the standard for piano trio performance over its 40-year history. The Philadelphia Chamber Music Society Players constitute a gifted resident group, and Musicians from Marlboro, a touring extension of the Vermont program, perform several times a season. Both are enlisted for more unusual musical groupings, such as piano quartets and string quintets.

Over the years, complementary series have been added. Especially popular is the piano recital series, whose artists have included Emanuel Ax, Richard Goode, Radu Lupu, Peter Serkin, András Schiff, and Mitsuko Uchida. Longtime audience members still remember the recital given by the great Polish pianist Mieczyslaw Horszowski at the age of 99. Another series, one of the very few nationwide, is devoted to the art song, attracting some of the world's most respected recitalists, including Elly Ameling, Thomas Hampson, Ewa Podleś, Hermann Prey, Frederica von Stade, and Benita Valente.

In recent years, PCMS has drawn in new audiences through its innovative Special Events Series. Among those taking part have been legendary pianist Marian McPartland with her trio; jazz greats Max Roach, McCoy Tyner, Chick Corea, and Joshua Redman; the four-woman *a cappella* group Anonymous 4; the husband-and-wife cabaret duo Joan Morris and William Bolcom; and the Albert McNeil Jubilee Singers, who specialize in African-American folk music.

The Society devotes much of its attention to the future of chamber music. A six-year program, sponsored by The Pew Charitable Trusts, enabled it to commission leading composers who live in our region to create new chamber works, whose world premieres were then given at regular concerts. Several of these compositions have been commercially recorded, and a few have won major prizes and awards.

The Philadelphia Chamber Music Society has strong community ties, collaborating with institutions such as the School District of Philadelphia, Temple University, The Curtis Institute of Music, The Musical Fund Society of Philadelphia, and the Samuel S. Fleisher Art Memorial. Some 35 educational programs are given each year to enrich the lives of area students, including master classes, seminars, free tickets, and free lectures before many of the regular concerts.

PCMS's artistic excellence and diverse and compelling programs have inspired much critical praise. The *Philadelphia Inquirer* has referred to its concerts as "musical Nirvana." ∎

THE GUARNERI STRING QUARTET. [PHOTO BY DOROTHEA VON HAEFTEN]

MIDORI. [PHOTO BY SUSAN JOHANN]

PETER NERO AND THE PHILLY POPS®

*L*aunched in 1979, Peter Nero and the Philly Pops® has made a name for itself both in its home city and around the world. Peter Nero, two-time Grammy Award-winning pianist, conductor, composer, and arranger, has led this orchestra with impeccable style and great skill, carefully crafting the ensemble into one that seamlessly combines music of different genres.

A recent *Washington Post* article called Nero "the epitome of the Pops conductor-performer." The Brooklyn-born Juilliard graduate is hailed for his solid musicianship, innovative programming, and warm, informal stage presence. His interpretations of George Gershwin, both as pianist and conductor, have received international acclaim. Nero has led some of the world's greatest orchestras and played in the finest concert halls, including The Kennedy Center in Washington, D.C., Royal Albert Hall in London, and the Concertgebouw in Amsterdam.

The POPS, endowed from the start with a talented group of instrumentalists from the musically rich Philadelphia area, has a vast repertoire, spanning the classics, jazz, blues, Broadway, Hollywood, ragtime, and rock 'n' roll. Thanks to Maestro Nero's expertise, their superb performances in all genres are unparalleled among pops orchestras. Each concert takes advantage of the diversity of the musicians and may include an improvised jam session or a bluegrass violin solo. The POPS is also proud of its own new vocal ensemble, The Voices of the Pops.

Opposite page: Peter Nero, Music Director and Conductor

Remaining photos: Peter Nero and the Philly Pops at the Academy of Music, May 2001. [Photos by Harvey Finkle]

Not many orchestras would dare to follow up a performance of the theme from the disco musical *The Wiz* with the last movement of the Beethoven Ninth Symphony. But, in its first season, Peter Nero and the Philly Pops did—and succeeded. "Miraculously," wrote a *Philadelphia Inquirer* music critic, "it worked!"

The ensemble made its Carnegie Hall debut in 1984 and has performed there as recently as 1997. In 1998, it had the honor of playing at NASA's 40th Anniversary Celebration in Washington, D.C., in which the featured work was Nero's dramatic, 17-minute composition entitled *Voyage into Space*, accompanied by spectacular multimedia visual effects. This spring, Peter Nero and the Philly Pops will make history by welcoming a true American hero, Senator John Glenn, in his first appearance with a symphony orchestra, narrating *Voyage into Space*.

Each season Nero performs some 100 concerts, about 20 of which are with the Philly Pops. He has released more than 65 recordings, many of them with full symphony orchestras, and others in collaboration with jazz legends such as Mel Tormé and Doc Severinsen. His association with RCA Records produced 23 albums in eight years, eight Grammy nominations, and two Grammy Awards. His subsequent move to Columbia Records resulted in two more Grammy nominations, as well as a million-selling album, *Summer of '42*, now available on CD. Nero has also made his mark in film, having composed the score for *Sunday in New York*, whose title song has become a staple among jazz musicians. The recipient of four honorary doctorates, Nero was honored by former Pennsylvania Governor Tom Ridge with the Distinguished Arts Award in 1999. In 2000, his orchestra was chosen to perform during the Republican National Convention in Philadelphia.

Under Nero, the Philly Pops has garnered a huge television audience, beginning in 1981 with a live coast-to-coast PBS broadcast. This summer the orchestra served as musical host of ABC's Independence Day 2001 star-studded patriotic celebration, broadcast live across the country from the steps of the Philadelphia Museum of Art. Another appearance in 1988 on CBS was part of "We the People," Philadelphia's bicentennial celebration of the U.S. Constitution. Also in 1988, the POPS was featured in "The Songs of Johnny Mercer: Too Marvelous for Words," a PBS special co-starring Peter Nero.

The POPS is also devoted to music education, which too often has been disappearing from school curricula. In 1998, Peter Nero launched "Jazz in the Schools," an outreach program in the tri-state area involving workshops and special performances. The U.S. Department of Education, recognizing the importance of this program, extended a grant in 2001 to further its efforts.

Peter Nero is a devotee and advocate of consumer electronics. If it's plugged in or battery-operated, say people who know him, then he has it. Clearly, The Kimmel Center, with its advanced technology, will be a perfect home for this adventurous programmer and his versatile musicians. ■

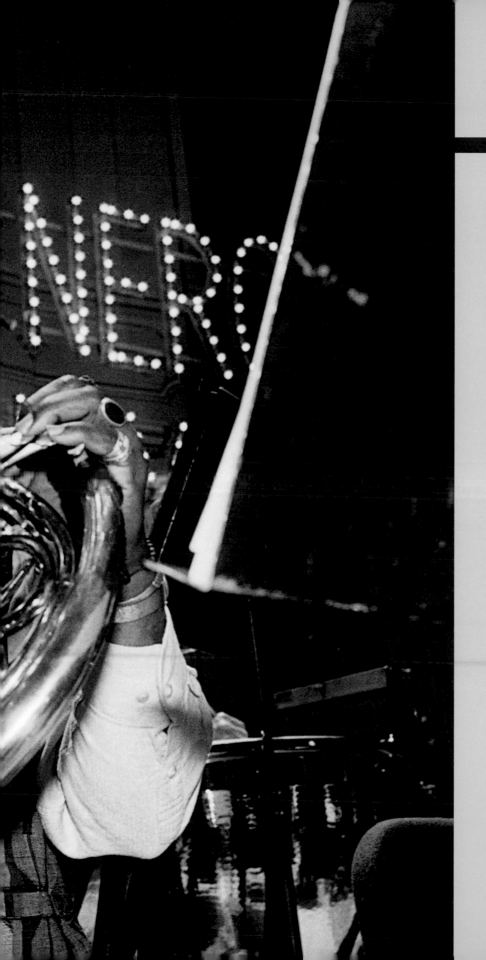

PETER NERO AND THE PHILLY POPS®
BOARD OF DIRECTORS/OFFICERS

An Overview

TOP: BENJAMIN FRANKLIN'S GLASS ARMONICA. [PHOTO © JAMES ABBOTT, COURTESY OF THE FRANKLIN INSTITUTE]

BOTTOM: THE MUSICAL FUND HALL, EIGHTH AND LOCUST STREETS, OPENED IN 1824. [PHOTO COURTESY OF THE PHILADELPHIA ORCHESTRA ASSOCIATION ARCHIVES]

PREVIOUS PAGE: STARTING IN 1930, THE PHILADELPHIA ORCHESTRA PLAYED A SUMMER SERIES AT THE ROBIN HOOD DELL IN FAIRMOUNT PARK. THE SERIES WAS LATER MOVED TO THE FREDRIC R. MANN CENTER FOR THE PERFORMING ARTS. [PHOTO BY JULES SCHICK, COURTESY OF THE PHILADELPHIA ORCHESTRA ASSOCIATION ARCHIVES]

Philadelphia was not only the cradle of American liberty, it was also a birthplace of the nation's performing arts. Classical music, opera, theater, and dance all took root here early on and flourished. Over the years, these art forms have gone through periods of popularity and growth, as well as decline, always recovering to reach new heights.

In recent years, Philadelphia's performing arts community has been hampered by a lack of performance space. With the opening of The Kimmel Center for the Performing Arts, people can look to a future in which these arts grow unimpeded. In the words of a 2001 *Philadelphia Inquirer* article, "Soon our town will be able to stop looking over its shoulder to see what New York has been doing."

A look at the rich history of performing arts in Philadelphia gives us clues to what we can expect in the future.

FROM SIMPLE BEGINNINGS TO THE DEVELOPMENT OF A GREAT ORCHESTRA

Musical instruments—viols, virginals (a small harpsichord), trumpets, and organs—were first brought to the Philadelphia region by German immigrants who settled here in the late 1600s. By 1703, there was an organ at Old Swedes' Church. Popular music also had an early start in Philadelphia; by 1724, strolling players were engaging in rope dancing, with the star performer being a clown called "Pickle Herring."

The city soon became a center for music education and innovation. Benjamin Franklin's press printed the city's first sheet music in 1729, and newspapers advertised music instruction as early as 1730. Franklin also developed a musical instrument called the "glass armonica," with graduated glasses mounted on a treadle-operated spindle. The instrument produces oddly pleasant tones when the musician touches the rims of the glasses with moistened fingers. To this day, the unique strains of this instrument can sometimes be heard at fairs and historical gatherings.

Francis Hopkinson, Franklin's friend and fellow signer of the Declaration of Independence, was also a composer and concert promoter. Among other musical events, Hopkinson produced an elaborate British masque (an early form of music theater) with students at the College of Philadelphia, later to become the University of Pennsylvania.

Philadelphia's first series of orchestral concerts was held in 1764. Thirty years later, an orchestra was formed to accompany the performance of ballad operas, another forerunner of today's musical theater.

A series of concerts in private homes led to the creation of the Musical Fund Society of Philadelphia in 1820, which quickly became the outstanding musical organization in the city. Today, it remains one of the oldest musical societies in the nation. The Society's 1821 debut featured no fewer than six conductors in an ambitious program that included Beethoven's Symphony No. 2. In 1824, the Society built its own concert hall at Eighth and Locust Streets, designed by the well-known architect William Strickland and much admired for its acoustics.

Taking its name from a Berlin ensemble that had given a series of concerts in Philadelphia in 1848, the Germania Orchestra was founded in 1856 under the leadership of Carl Sentz. The city's first significant resident orchestra, it provided Philadelphians with regular concerts during the orchestra season and promenade concerts in summer.

A major name in American orchestral circles during the late 1800s was conductor Theodore Thomas, whose frenetic tours with his eponymous orchestra brought him to Philadelphia annually. Thomas was named music director of the nation's grand and ambitious Centennial Exposition, held in 1876 in Fairmount Park. His commissioning of a non-American—the German operatic composer Richard Wagner, no less—to write the *Grand Centennial Inaugural March* was the cause of much grousing. Wagner's piece was largely a disappointment—even the composer said, "The best thing about that composition was the money I got for it." French composer Jacques Offenbach became the musical hero of the celebration, charming audiences with his lighter fare.

ABOVE: THEODORE THOMAS, WHOSE ORCHESTRA VISITED PHILADELPHIA ANNUALLY DURING THE LATE 1800S, WAS MUSIC DIRECTOR OF THE CENTENNIAL EXPOSITION IN 1876. [PHOTO COURTESY OF THE PHILADELPHIA ORCHESTRA ASSOCIATION ARCHIVES]

When Thomas's orchestra ceased coming to Philadelphia, the loss was partly compensated for by visits from the Boston Symphony Orchestra and the New York Symphony Orchestra, among other fine ensembles. Feeling the need for a more permanent orchestra, three Philadelphians—composer William Gilchrist, opera conductor Gustav Hinrichs, and choral director Henry Gordon Thunder—organized the amateur Symphony Society of Philadelphia in 1893, which played three concerts a year at the Academy of Music. In 1899, they engaged Fritz Scheel from Lübeck, Germany, to direct the series, paving the way for the formation of The Philadelphia Orchestra.

The Orchestra developed from two successful concerts in 1900 to benefit the families of Philippine war victims, with Scheel at the podium. The first performance of the newly formed professional ensemble took place on November 16, 1900. During his seven-year tenure as the Orchestra's first Music Director, Scheel brought in a number of fine players trained in Europe, as was standard practice among American orchestras at the time.

In 1907, Scheel passed the baton to Carl Pohlig, a fellow German who had worked under composers Franz Liszt and Gustav Mahler. Under Pohlig's leadership, the young Orchestra expanded its schedule, playing 86 concerts per year, 18 of them to audiences outside Philadelphia.

With the arrival of the golden-haired, charismatic Leopold Stokowski in 1912, The Philadelphia Orchestra began to win the international renown that it has maintained to this day. Stokowski's successors have been three of the most illustrious musicians of their time: Eugene Ormandy, Riccardo Muti, and Wolfgang Sawallisch, each of whom has stamped the ensemble with his own unique personality. Poised to take on the music directorship in 2003–4, with the retirement of the much-loved Sawallisch, is Christoph Eschenbach, who has had a brilliant career both as a solo pianist and as music director of the esteemed Houston Symphony.

During the summer, Philadelphia audiences have been fortunate to hear their favorite orchestra in the open-air setting of Fairmount Park, first at the Robin Hood Dell and now at the Fredric R. Mann Center for the Performing Arts. Along with the Orchestra, which often plays with renowned soloists, the Mann hosts a varied spectrum of events, including Broadway shows, jazz, children's theater, and innovative multimedia opera productions.

Among Philadelphia's smaller instrumental ensembles is The Chamber Orchestra of Philadelphia, a Resident Company of The Kimmel Center. Founded in 1964 by Marc Mostovoy, it was the second full-time chamber orchestra to be formed in the United States. Orchestra 2001 and Network for New Music are both highly respected for their performances of contemporary music. The ensembles Philomel, Philadelphia Classical Symphony, and Piffaro perform early music on period instruments.

For anyone who doubts that students can sound like a major orchestra, hearing the Curtis Symphony Orchestra's annual series of concerts at the Academy of Music proves otherwise. Formed in 1924, the Curtis Institute of Music is one of the world's great conservatories. It grew out of the Settlement School in South Philadelphia, founded in 1908 to provide music education and performance to the communities it serves. Another ensemble for young musicians (aged 10 to 21) is the Philadelphia Youth Orchestra, founded in 1939, which has toured extensively around the world.

Effortlessly bridging the worlds of classical and popular music is Peter Nero and the Philly Pops°, a Resident Company of The Kimmel Center, a group that has been playing Beethoven, Broadway, jazz, and everything in between for more than a quarter-century.

THE INTIMATE FORM OF CHAMBER MUSIC

Small instrumental ensembles have existed in Philadelphia since the mid-18th century. The first known chamber music series in the colonies began here in 1757, with General George Washington among those who attended.

During the winter of 1816–17, string quartets by composers such as Beethoven and Boccherini were performed for select gatherings in local homes. In 1830, the Apollo Society was founded to give chamber music concerts, attracting new admirers to this intimate form. Eagerly awaited in the early 20th century were frequent visits from groups such as the Kneisel String Quartet. When that group disbanded, the Chamber Music Association was founded, bringing many of the best international ensembles to Philadelphia.

Among the homegrown ensembles of note was the Curtis String Quartet. Formed in 1927 by students at The Curtis Institute of Music, the Quartet performed for more than half a century, touring the world and recording. So valuable were their instruments that they were once locked in a midwestern jail for safekeeping while the Quartet members took a movie break.

The Philadelphia Museum of Art was the site of several chamber music concerts sponsored by the Curtis Institute. A six-concert series in 1928–29 drew 30,000 people—hardly the intimate gathering ideal for this form, but gratifying nonetheless.

A fine chamber music series ran between 1948 and 1977 at the Free Library on Benjamin Franklin Parkway, featuring the Juilliard and Curtis string quartets, as well as the Philadelphia Woodwind Quintet, composed of Philadelphia Orchestra musicians. Another series,

the Coffee Concerts, emerged in 1959. When these series were discontinued, chamber music performances grew infrequent.

Fortunately, in 1986, the Philadelphia Chamber Music Society—now a Resident Company at The Kimmel Center—was born. Starting modestly, it has become the most successful and comprehensive series of its kind in the nation, consistently exciting audiences with an exceptional and eclectic repertoire.

The Philadelphia Orchestra initiated its own chamber music series in the 1980s, which started in the Academy of Music Ballroom and will continue in The Kimmel Center's Perelman Theater. Here, enthusiastic audiences hear the Orchestra's fine musicians in works that showcase their individual instruments. Among the city's other Orchestra-staffed chamber groups are 1807 & Friends and The Philadelphia Chamber Ensemble.

PHILADELPHIA TURNS OPERATIC

The earliest known performance of opera in Philadelphia was of the British ballad opera *Hob in the Well* in 1754. The Old American Opera Company, Plumstead's Warehouse, and the Southwark Theatre were early venues for this type of entertainment, with American ballad operas being composed as early as 1767. A major influence at the end of the 18th century was British-born Benjamin Carr, who was a composer, singer, and presenter.

Philadelphia's enthusiasm for Italian opera was ignited in the early 19th century by Lorenzo da Ponte, Mozart's brilliant librettist, whose amorous, political, and financial misadventures caused him to flee Europe for the United States. Soon Verdi, Mozart, and Bellini were the rage. In 1845 the first American opera was staged in Philadelphia. Alas, it was a paltry effort by William Henry Fry called *Leonora* and expired soon after its birth.

With the rise of interest in opera came the desire for a proper opera house. The Academy of Music opened in 1857 to great fanfare, and was quickly recognized as the finest venue in the nation. The first opera to be heard there was Verdi's *Il trovatore*, just four years after its premiere. The Metropolitan Opera made a first appearance at the Academy in 1884, performing Meyerbeer's *Les Huguenots*. Soon the Met was bringing several operas annually to Philadelphia audiences, a highlight of the musical season that lasted until 1968, when rising costs made the venture prohibitive.

RIGHT: OPENED IN 1924, THE CURTIS INSTITUTE OF MUSIC IS ONE OF THE WORLD'S GREAT CONSERVATORIES, AND MANY OF ITS GRADUATES HAVE BECOME MEMBERS OF THE PHILADELPHIA ORCHESTRA. [PHOTO COURTESY OF THE CURTIS INSTITUTE OF MUSIC]

An early and brazen challenge to both the Met and the Academy came from impresario Oscar Hammerstein, a devotee of French opera, who built a rival 4,000-seat theater in Philadelphia. When the Philadelphia Opera House opened in 1908—on the same night as the Met's season opener—patrons could not decide which opera to attend. Some even scurried from one to another at intermission. Ever the showman, Hammerstein scandalized the city a few years later with a performance of

ABOVE: SOPRANO ADELINA PATTI FIRST PERFORMED IN PHILADELPHIA AT THE AGE OF SEVEN. IN 1860, SHE SANG FOR THE VISITING PRINCE OF WALES (AND FUTURE EDWARD VII) AT THE ACADEMY OF MUSIC. [PHOTO COURTESY OF THE COLLECTION OF GIRVICE ARCHER, JR.]

Richard Strauss's *Salome* in which Mary Garden shed her seven veils, to the dismay of the city's ministerial associations. Hammerstein's company eventually failed, and the city's operatic loyalty reverted to the Met and the Academy of Music.

After World War I, local opera companies began to form, including the Philadelphia Civic Opera in 1924, and the Philadelphia Grand Opera Company in 1926. The latter company joined with that champion of 20th-century music, Leopold Stokowski, in a major undertaking: the American premiere of Alban Berg's shocking *Wozzeck*, with The Philadelphia Orchestra in the pit.

To fill the void left by the departure of New York's Metropolitan Opera from Philadelphia, the Lyric and Grand Opera companies merged in 1976 to form the Opera Company of Philadelphia, now a Resident Company at the Academy of Music. Under the leadership of Margaret Ann Everitt, the Opera Company increased its international presence through a voice competition developed with the great tenor Luciano Pavarotti, and through several fine television productions, one of which won an Emmy Award. Robert B. Driver took over the company in 1991, bringing it artistic growth, financial stability, and an ever-multiplying subscriber base.

The Pennsylvania Opera Theater, founded and led by Barbara Silverstein, came into being in the mid-1970s. Specializing in little-known and contemporary operas, sung in English, the company gave opportunities to younger singers and was popular with Philadelphia opera lovers for almost two decades.

Philadelphia has contributed major names to the world of opera. The Italian-born Gian Carlo Menotti, who studied at The Curtis Institute of Music, composed two operas that premiered here: *Amelia Goes to the Ball* and *The Consul*. Two of the most legendary vocalists of the 20th century were Philadelphia-born. Marian Anderson, the lustrous-voiced contralto and humanitarian whose grace and strength helped open the doors of opera to fellow African Americans, was a South Philadelphian. And so was Mario Lanza, the famed tenor and actor who is best known for playing the title role in the film *The Great Caruso*.

African Americans have contributed to Philadelphia's opera scene for well over a century. In 1860, Elizabeth Taylor Greenfield, a former slave and self-taught musician, formed The Black Opera Troupe. A century later, Sister Mary Elise, a septuagenarian nun of great energy and dedication, founded Opera Ebony; this fine company subsequently became Opera North.

Three of the city's educational institutions present opera of professional quality: the Academy of Vocal Arts, dating from 1933 and devoted to training opera singers; Temple University's Esther Boyer College of Music; and The Curtis Institute of Music.

The city also boasts the Savoy Company, the oldest amateur theater group in the world dedicated solely to producing works by Gilbert and Sullivan. New to the scene is the Opera Theater of Philadelphia, which features up-and-coming directors, designers, and singers.

LEFT: PHILADELPHIA-BORN CONTRALTO MARIAN ANDERSON. [PHOTO COURTESY OF THE FREE LIBRARY OF PHILADELPHIA, PRINT AND PICTURE COLLECTION]

RIGHT: SOUTH PHILADELPHIA-BORN TENOR MARIO LANZA, WHO BROUGHT OPERA TO THE SILVER SCREEN. [PHOTO COURTESY OF THE FREE LIBRARY OF PHILADELPHIA, PRINT AND PICTURE COLLECTION]

WITH ONE VOICE: CHORUS IN PHILADELPHIA

Choral music, as performed by amateurs, has flourished in Philadelphia from the end of the 18th century. The city's various religious groups were a focal point of this activity. A large number of African-American churches banded to form the African Harmonic Society of Philadelphia in 1827, organized to promote church music in the black community. This strong tradition ultimately led to the gospel phenomenon of the 20th century.

The all-male Orpheus Club, founded in 1872, is the oldest Philadelphia vocal ensemble still in existence. The Mendelssohn Club was formed two years later, in 1874, and remains a vital part of Philadelphia's choral scene. Beginning as an eight-voice male chorus, it soon increased in size and added women. In 1916, when Leopold Stokowski and The Philadelphia Orchestra gave the American premiere of Mahler's Symphony No. 8 (Symphony of a Thousand), the Mendelssohn Club provided more than 300 of the 950 choristers. So wildly popular was the event that scalpers drove ticket prices from ten cents to $100.

Other still vital ensembles were established in the 20th century. Singing City, started in 1948 by Dr. Elaine Brown, became known internationally for its artistic excellence and its commitment to peace and social justice. The Philadelphia Singers, created by Michael Korn and currently headed by David Hayes, first performed in 1971; it is currently the resident chorus of The Philadelphia Orchestra and has had the honor of performing with the New York Philharmonic twice at the Lincoln Center Festival. It has performed in a number of world and American premieres and recorded several CDs.

ABOVE: FOR THE PHILADELPHIA ORCHESTRA'S 1916 U.S. PREMIERE OF MAHLER'S SYMPHONY NO. 8, MORE THAN A THOUSAND MUSICIANS WERE ASSEMBLED ON THE ACADEMY STAGE, INCLUDING 950 CHORISTERS AND EIGHT VOCAL SOLOISTS. [PHOTO COURTESY OF THE PHILADELPHIA ORCHESTRA ASSOCIATION ARCHIVES]

BELOW: THE MENDELSSOHN CLUB OF PHILADELPHIA, FOUNDED 1874, IS ONE OF AMERICA'S OLDEST MUSICAL ENSEMBLES. [PHOTO © 2000 JOHN LEWIS SHIPMAN, COURTESY OF THE MENDELSSOHN CLUB OF PHILADELPHIA]

Pennsylvania Pro Musica, The Choral Arts Society of Philadelphia, and the Music Group of Philadelphia are other significant contributors to the choral scene, bringing a vast repertoire, from medieval to modern, to Philadelphia audiences.

THEATER TAKES CENTER STAGE

The first permanent theater in America was Philadelphia's Southwark, built in 1766, an oil-lit, rough red brick and wood structure. Here Thomas Godfrey's *The Prince of Parthia* became the first play by an American to be professionally staged. For a quarter of a century the Southwark was the only real

theater in the city. The Continental Congress forbade all entertainment during the Revolution, but occupying forces under General Howe had a fine old time mounting plays at the Southwark and staging music on barges.

After the Revolution, theatrical entertainment grew in popularity, and in 1794 the Chestnut Street Theatre, considered to be the most handsome playhouse in the country, was built. America's first circus opened in Philadelphia in 1793. Another circus building opened in 1809 and eventually became the Walnut Street Theatre. This remains the oldest continuously operated theater in the English-speaking world and, several restorations later, is heralded as a National Historic Landmark.

Among those to perform at the Walnut was Philadelphia native Edwin Forrest, the first great American tragedian. He made his professional debut there at age 14, at a time when many thought that America was too backward to produce great actors. By age 30, however, Forrest was a star on both sides of the Atlantic. In 1842, Charlotte Cushman took over management of the theater, a highly unusual achievement for a woman at that time.

Other major names in American theater associated with Philadelphia included three siblings, all actors, Lionel, Ethel, and John Barrymore, whose actress grandmother managed the Arch Street Theatre.

Gradually the city lost its foremost position in the theater world to New York and, by the 1920s, became known as a tryout town for Broadway-bound productions. The theory was that if a play could survive in Philadelphia, it would have a long run on Broadway.

Built in 1918 was the Shubert Theater, which attracted such legendary actors as Helen Hayes, Katharine Hepburn, and Sir Laurence Olivier, and became an important Broadway roadhouse. The Shubert was later renamed the Merriam and restored by its present owner, the 125-year-old University of the Arts, a neighbor to The Kimmel Center. The Merriam is also used for many of the University's productions.

Community theater arose early in Philadelphia and grew in significance as touring Broadway shows declined. Plays and Players, an amateur theater club formed in 1911, is one of the nation's oldest theater clubs and operates its own theater on Delancey Street. Society Hill Playhouse, opened in 1959, is the city's oldest professional off-Broadway theater. The Philadelphia Theatre Company, formed in

LEFT: THE CHESTNUT STREET THEATRE, C. 1854. [PHOTO COURTESY OF THE FREE LIBRARY OF PHILADELPHIA, PRINT AND PICTURE COLLECTION]

ABOVE, LEFT: EDWIN FORREST, THE FIRST AMERICAN ACTOR TO ACHIEVE SUCCESS ON BOTH SIDES OF THE ATLANTIC. [PHOTO COURTESY OF THE FREE LIBRARY OF PHILADELPHIA, THEATRE COLLECTION]

ABOVE, RIGHT: ACTRESS CHARLOTTE CUSHMAN, WHO MANAGED THE WALNUT STREET THEATRE IN THE 1840S. [PHOTO © BETTMANN/CORBIS]

BELOW, LEFT: THE ARDEN THEATRE COMPANY MAINSTAGE IN OLD CITY. [PHOTO BY BARRY HALKIN, HALKIN PHOTOGRAPH & IMAGES, COURTESY OF THE ARDEN THEATRE COMPANY]

BELOW, RIGHT: THE SOCIETY HILL PLAYHOUSE. [PHOTO COURTESY OF THE SOCIETY HILL PLAYHOUSE]

1974, gained full Equity status in 1981 and continues to premiere bold new works by contemporary playwrights.

One company that has achieved world recognition is the Wilma, which was started as an experimental theater group in 1973. Czechoslovakians Blanka and Jiri Zizka took over artistic leadership of the company in 1981, expanding its audience dramatically through their inventive and provocative staging of works by such major playwrights as Bertolt Brecht, Athol Fugard, and Tom Stoppard. Its new home on the Avenue of the Arts, opened in 1996, is the first professional theater built in Center City since 1928.

Another exciting part of the theater scene is the Arden Theatre Company, founded in 1988, and winner of twelve Barrymore awards for its innovative presentations. Opening in 1999 on the Avenue of the Arts was the Prince Music Theater, formerly American Music Theater Festival, which has brought many American or world premieres to Philadelphia. Groups such as the InterAct Theatre Company are devoted to experimental theater based around the issues relevant to our time.

The former home of actor Edwin Forrest on the Avenue of the Arts is now the headquarters of Freedom Theatre, the oldest African-American theater in Pennsylvania. Founded by John E. Allen more than 30 years ago, this professional theater offers about 150 performances a year and runs a performing arts training program whose alumni now number more than 10,000.

Youth is further served by American Theater Arts for Youth, a Resident Company of The Kimmel Center, and the nation's largest presenter of professional, curriculum-based theater for children. The University of Pennsylvania's Annenberg Center for the Performing Arts, a multidisciplinary performance venue, provides a rich spectrum of entertainment, including children's theater.

ON THEIR TOES: THE DANCE HERITAGE

Dance was part of Philadelphia's cultural life in the colonial era. In 1748, the Philadelphia Dance Assembly, which combined amateur and professional performances at private gatherings, was founded at the City Tavern. Discontinued and then reconstructed, the Assemblies continued well into the 19th century.

Philadelphia can claim the nation's two first ballet dancers of renown, Mary Ann Lee, born here in 1823, and Augusta Maywood, born two years later. Both studied with Paul Hazard, a retired dancer who had trained at the Paris Opera, and made their debuts at the Chestnut

Street Theatre in 1837. Not surprisingly, a rivalry developed between them. Maywood was probably the superior dancer and the better known internationally, but Lee possessed the greater charm and beauty. Traveling to France, she brought back productions of the great Romantic ballets and introduced them to Philadelphia audiences.

The city became quite sophisticated in its dance tastes with visits during the 19th and early 20th centuries from leading ballet, modern, and ballroom dancers, among them Isadora Duncan, Anna Pavlova, Vernon and Irene Castle, Ted Shawn, Ruth St. Denis, and Paul Draper.

Classical dance was given a huge boost in Philadelphia when native-born Catherine Littlefield founded the Littlefield Ballet (later renamed Philadelphia Ballet) in 1935, with her mother as co-director. The company was an outgrowth of their ballet school, which continued to be an influential force in American ballet through the 1940s. Littlefield's company was the first in the nation to be composed entirely of and directed by Americans, and the first to tour Europe. Its

CATHERINE LITTLEFIELD, FOUNDER OF THE PHILADELPHIA BALLET. [PHOTO COURTESY OF THE FREE LIBRARY OF PHILADELPHIA, THEATRE COLLECTION]

core repertoire was classical, but American themes—unique for that time—were introduced as well. After the company disbanded, Littlefield broke into New York's music theater, one of her creations being a routine for 90 dancers perched on bicycles.

Modern dance came to Philadelphia in the late 1920s and became popular in the next decade. One of the major dance performances of this period was the stage premiere of Igor Stravinsky's *The Rite of Spring*, with the great Martha Graham as soloist, and Leopold Stokowski conducting The Philadelphia Orchestra. Jazz dancing developed somewhat later, thanks to such artists as Marion Cuyjet, Sydney King, and Essie Marie Dorsey.

The Philadelphia Dance Academy was formed in 1946 by Nadia Chilkovsky, a protégée of Isadora Duncan. Subsequently, British choreographer Anthony Tudor formed a small ballet company. Pennsylvania Ballet, now a Resident Company at the Academy of Music, had its first Philadelphia performance in 1964, sponsored by the prestigious Philadelphia Art Alliance. At the helm of the new company was Barbara Weisberger, with the legendary George Balanchine as artistic director. Quickly, Pennsylvania Ballet became a leader in the regional ballet movement.

Another name that is woven into the city's dance history is Judith Jamison, born here in 1944. Trained in ballet, tap, jazz and modern dance, the tall, long-limbed and elegant dancer/choreographer is best known for her work with the Alvin Ailey American Dance Theater, where she starred for many years, taking over the company's artistic leadership after Ailey's death.

Among this city's African-American dance pioneers is Joan Myers Brown, founder of PHILADANCO (short for Philadelphia Dance Company) in 1970. Brown had earlier opened a school in West Philadelphia to train black dancers. Today PHILADANCO, which is still under her committed leadership and joins The Kimmel Center's Resident Companies, is known around the world for its intense and powerful performances.

Modern dance is clearly on the upswing in Philadelphia. After a rocky period during the 1980s caused by cutbacks in funding, the city, according to the *Philadelphia Inquirer*, can claim a "dance environment that is virtually unique in the country," with such innovative companies as Rennie Harris's Puremovement, Court, Headlong Dance Theater, and Group Motion bringing everything from flamenco to tap to gravity-defying productions with ropes and rigging. A dance collective called Kumquat has allowed for many innovative partnerships between companies and choreographers.

POPULAR MUSIC: FROM JAZZ TO ROCK, FOLK TO GOSPEL
Strumming street guitarists have serenaded Philadelphians since the 1700s, when their instruments were made from gourds. With the American Revolution came a growing interest in martial music, parades, and theater music. Tavern fiddlers and church organists alike played lilts and jigs.

Francis (Frank) Johnson, a Martinique native born in 1809, was a songwriter, music educator, violinist, bugler, and the most sought-after bandleader of his time. Having performed in Europe, he settled in Philadelphia, where his band played for balls, private parties, military regiments, and celebratory events. Among the popular European

THE INTERIOR OF THE LINCOLN THEATRE AT BROAD AND LOMBARD, WHERE VAUDEVILLE ACTS AS WELL AS JAZZ AND RHYTHM-AND-BLUES PERFORMERS TOOK THE STAGE. [PHOTO COURTESY OF GLAZER COLLECTION/ATHENAEUM OF PHILADELPHIA.]

traditions he introduced here were waltzes and English-style promenade concerts. His was the first American band to tour Europe.

In the latter part of the 19th century, a number of African-American songwriters rose to prominence. Among them were John Clemens (whose "Coal Black Rose," dating from 1829, was the first widely popular American song), Aaron Conner, James Hemmenway, Isaac Hazzard, and William App. Philadelphia also became a center of minstrel shows, vaudeville, and tap dancing.

In the first half of the 20th century, many movie houses presented both films and staged shows. Big band jazz and rhythm-and-blues stars like Pearl Bailey, Bessie Smith, Cab Calloway, Duke Ellington, and Della Reese performed at venues such as the Earle Theater, Lincoln Theatre, and Royal Theater. At the Royal, Fats Waller would sometimes play the organ between movie features. In 1998,

DRUMMER PHILLY JOE JONES, WHO PLAYED WITH THE FIRST MILES DAVIS QUINTET. [PHOTO COURTESY OF METRONOME/HULTON/ARCHIVE]

this historic South Street landmark (built in 1920) was saved from demolition, and plans are underway for refurbishing it as a live performance theater.

In the 1940s and 1950s, lured by clubs like the Blue Note, the Showboat, Peps, Sahara, and the Latin Casino, such greats as Louis Armstrong, Gene Krupa, Harry James, Lionel Hampton, Benny Goodman, and Frank Sinatra appeared in Philadelphia. Philadelphia has also had its share of homegrown talent in such legendary musicians as McCoy Tyner, Stan Getz, Philly Joe Jones, Odean Pope, Kenny Barron, Joe Venuti, and Shirley Scott. John Coltrane, Nina Simone, and Grover Washington, Jr., came of age as performers here after moving to the city early in their careers. Crucial to the development of jazz in the city was the Black Musicians' Union, founded in 1935, which, 30 years later, became The Philadelphia Clef Club of Jazz. Now on the Avenue of the Arts, the Clef Club is the first facility in the nation created as a jazz institution.

In the decades after World War II, Philadelphia became a mecca for popular music. Teen idols Frankie Avalon, Fabian, Bobby Rydell, and Chubby ("The Twist") Checker hailed from South Philadelphia, and rock 'n' roll pioneer Bill Haley, whose 1955 hit "Rock Around the Clock" has sold more than 22 million copies worldwide, was from nearby Chester. These performers, along with such rock legends as Buddy Holly and Ritchie Valens, appeared as guests on Dick Clark's *American Bandstand*, broadcast live from WFIL's TV studios at 46th and Market starting in 1956. The show, which featured local teenagers

demonstrating such dances as the Slop, the Calypso, the Bunny Hop, and the Snowball, went national in 1957 and aired coast-to-coast on ABC for four decades (though starting in 1960 it was broadcast from Hollywood).

The late 1950s and early 1960s brought the folk music revival, and once again, Philadelphia was at the forefront with clubs

ABOVE: DICK CLARK INTERVIEWS SINGER BOBBY RYDELL ON *AMERICAN BANDSTAND*, WHICH BROADCAST FROM PHILADELPHIA STARTING IN 1956. [PHOTO COURTESY OF HULTON/ARCHIVE]

and coffeehouses such as the Gilded Cage and Second Fret. A dedicated group of local folk enthusiasts formed the Philadelphia Folksong Society in 1957, now the largest organization of its kind in North America. In addition to offering concerts, workshops, and scholarships, the Society also hosts the internationally known Philadelphia Folk Festival. Held outdoors each year in Schwenksville, the festival just celebrated its 40th anniversary and continues to bring the finest in folk music to the area.

LEFT: PATTI LABELLE SINGS THE NATIONAL ANTHEM AT A 2001 PHILADELPHIA 76ERS PLAYOFF GAME. [PHOTO © AFP/CORBIS]

RIGHT: TEDDY PENDERGRASS, ONE OF THE SUPERSTARS TO EMERGE FROM GAMBLE AND HUFF'S INTERNATIONAL RECORDS STUDIO ON SOUTH BROAD STREET. [PHOTO © NEAL PRESTON/CORBIS]

The Philadelphia Orchestra is credited with creating the "Philadelphia Sound," but in the 1970s another type of "Philly Sound" was being pioneered right across the street from the Academy of Music, at Kenneth Gamble

THE PHILADELPHIA FOLK FESTIVAL HAS DRAWN GREAT PERFORMERS AND LARGE AUDIENCES FOR FOUR DECADES. [PHOTO COURTESY OF THE PHILADELPHIA FOLKSONG SOCIETY]

and Leon Huff's *Philadelphia International Records.* In 1971, this Philadelphia songwriter/producer team began to define their trademark sound—a melodic style of urban soul that featured silky-smooth vocals atop funky bass lines and lush, string-laden orchestration—which would come to characterize the decade. Gamble and Huff scored one hit after another with artists such as Jerry Butler, Billy Paul, the O'Jays, the Intruders, Harold Melvin and the Blue Notes, and Teddy Pendergrass.

Philadelphia's Patti LaBelle, whose chart-topping career began in 1962 as the lead singer of the Bluebelles, has continued to achieve critical and commercial success across four decades, first with her band, LaBelle, and then in more than 30 solo records showcasing her soaring vocal style, influenced by the strong gospel element that underlies much soul, jazz, and rock music. The immensely popular vocal group Boyz II Men and newcomer Jill Scott are carrying Philadelphia's strong R&B tradition into a new era.

In the late 1980s and 1990s, rap music found a distinctly Philadelphia voice in Schoolly D and DJ Jazzy Jeff and the Fresh Prince. The latter duo helped bring rap music into the mainstream, and the "Fresh Prince" himself, Will Smith, has become a major star on television and in film without parting from his hip-hop roots. More recently, the Roots, with their poetic topical lyrics and infectious beats, have emerged as a strong voice in contemporary hip hop.

In addition to the many national and international stars whose careers have been launched here, Philadelphia boasts a vibrant local music scene across every genre, and on any given night one can find jazz, rock, folk, hip-hop, reggae, and electronic dance music being showcased in clubs across the city.

INNOVATION AND TRADITION

Philadelphia long had the reputation—in part, perhaps, deserved—of being a staid city, one that did not welcome change. Today the scene is quite different. While remaining faithful to the old, Philadelphia is also open to the new.

In 1969 an organization was founded by Gerry Givnish that revitalized the South Street neighborhood and became the foremost outpost of alternative performances and visual arts in Philadelphia. This was the Painted Bride Art Center, which today maintains an innovative mix of music, dance, poetry, and the visual arts that is recognized nationwide.

Almost two decades later, the Philadelphia Fringe Festival came onto the scene in Old City, another neighborhood that has seen remarkable growth. In 2000 the 16-day extravaganza attracted 35,000 to its hundreds of events, held within a few mere blocks. From trapeze artists to puppet shows, political comedy to grand opera, stilt walkers to a Shakespearean play set in a child's wading pool, there was no end to the surprises.

But if votes were taken for Philadelphia's most festive and distinctive mixed-media event, the hands-down winner would probably be the oldest one of all: the annual Mummers Parade, held on New Year's Day. Its origins lie in the customs of the early Swedes, with further inspirations from other ethnic groups, including Philadelphia's Welsh, Swiss, English, German, and African-American communities.

First sanctioned by the city in 1901, the 10,000 Mummers—mostly men but with a growing number of women—march along Market Street (previously Broad Street) for ten hours, frequently in frigid weather, doing a curious bent-knee dance known as the "Mummers' Strut." As many as 100,000 spectators line the streets to gape at the huge floats and elaborate costumes full of feathers and sequins, while the sounds of massed banjos, saxophones, string basses, and glockenspiels fill the air.

Alternately raucous, sentimental, dignified, satirical, colorful, and just plain fun, the Mummers Parade is a true community event and a wonderful way to usher in the New Year. It is somehow fitting that the Mummers, Philly's oldest, were among those chosen to usher in Philly's newest, The Kimmel Center for the Performing Arts, in December of 2001. ■

A 20TH-CENTURY DREAM BECOMES A 21ST-CENTURY REALITY:
A HISTORY AND TOUR OF THE KIMMEL CENTER

A 20th-Century Dream Becomes a 21st-Century Reality

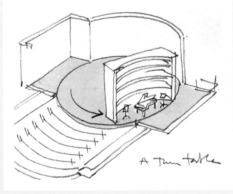

Friday and Saturday evening, December 14–15, 2001. Throngs of eager concertgoers and curious onlookers line Philadelphia's Avenue of the Arts. All eyes are on a glowing, glass-enclosed building whose redbrick exterior leads upward to a soaring barrel-vaulted roof of glass and steel, 150 feet high at the center. It is a marvel of engineering: 8,600 panes of tinted glass enclosing the building in an accordion-like pattern and held firm by a framework of structural steel. Already the glass vault is a Philadelphia landmark, as much a part of the city as the statue of William Penn standing guard above City Hall, or the skyscrapers One and Two Liberty Place.

The Kimmel Center for the Performing Arts has evolved from dream to reality.

Looking inside—this building invites looking both in and out—we see a magnificent interior courtyard, Commonwealth Plaza. This vast but welcoming civic space functions as an indoor public square, open from morning to night, where all are welcome.

Near the Spruce Street entrance is the curved exterior of the intimate Perelman Theater, atop which is the verdant, tree-lined Rooftop Garden. Continuing through the Plaza we reach Verizon Hall, a 2,500-seat, cello-shaped venue whose aesthetic beauty, guests will soon learn, is matched by its acoustical excellence.

The qualities of light and lightness that characterize The Kimmel Center are due in large measure to the extensive use of glass. Indeed, there is enough of it to cover 3.6 acres. A glass-and-steel vertical elevator tower leads to a sky-bridge, from which we can see every level from floor to ceiling. Even the walls of the vault at both ends of the Center are glass—massive panels hanging from vertical cables designed to sway gently (and safely) with the wind.

This distinctly 21st-century creation is a truly interactive space, a worthy centerpiece for Philadelphia's renamed and refurbished Avenue of the Arts.

BACK TO THE BEGINNING

The Kimmel Center's origins can be traced to the beginning of the 20th century, when the newly formed Philadelphia Orchestra moved into the Academy of Music. Known fondly to generations of music lovers as "The Grand Old Lady of Locust Street," the elegant Academy, built in 1857, was modeled loosely on the renowned La Scala opera

THE REGIONAL PERFORMING ARTS CENTER

house in Milan, Italy. With its proscenium arch and orchestra pit, the ornate house is well suited to opera and ballet, but it presents challenges for a symphony orchestra, which requires acoustical warmth, immediacy, and a different kind of resonance. Nor is it visually ideal for symphonic performance, since the proscenium stage, designed to accommodate large sets, separates onstage musicians from their audiences.

As early as 1908 plans were drawn (and subsequently dropped) for a new 2,800-seat auditorium. In the late 1920s, Leopold Stokowski, who elevated The Philadelphia Orchestra to international fame, talked about his hope for a "great temple of music dedicated to the people." His most generous benefactor, the publisher Cyrus Curtis, bought a site for such a hall, but the project ended with Curtis's death and the subsequent Depression.

Still, the Orchestra dreamed. And then, in 1986, during the tenure of Music Director Riccardo Muti, the Orchestra's Board of Directors authorized the design and construction of a new concert hall. Real estate was gradually acquired at Broad and Spruce Streets, where The Kimmel Center now stands. The well-known Philadelphia architectural firm Venturi, Scott Brown and Associates drew up plans for a $60 million hall, and the Orchestra selected Russell Johnson and his firm, Artec Consultants, as the project's acoustician. New developments, however, would soon change the scope of the project.

A MAYOR, A DONOR, AND A DEVELOPER

Edward G. Rendell was elected mayor of Philadelphia in 1992. During his two terms, he stewarded the city into an era of unsurpassed growth and civic pride and recognized Philadelphia's potential to become an international center for the arts. The focal point of this transformation would be a mile-long stretch of South Broad Street, from City Hall to Washington Avenue, already rich in cultural and educational institutions and performance venues. With a repaved avenue and new sidewalks, streetlights, and landscaping, the area now called the Avenue of the Arts was born.

In the summer of 1993, the Commonwealth of Pennsylvania, under Governor Robert Casey, pledged $60 million to the Avenue of the Arts initiative, $35 million of which was allocated to The Philadelphia Orchestra's plan for a new concert hall.

That year, the project also received a much-needed boost in the form of a major gift from entrepreneur Sidney Kimmel. A Philadelphia native and founder of Jones Apparel Group, Kimmel donated $12 million toward an Orchestra hall, generously adding $3 million more when the scope of the project was expanded. Since that time, additional donations from Kimmel have brought his total commitment to the Center to $30 million. He remains the Center's largest individual donor, and its name honors his early and crucial philanthropy.

Also planned for the Avenue was a smaller venue to house several fine performance groups that lacked permanent homes. It was to be built on City-owned land, with $8 million in Commonwealth funds already committed to the project. But the Mayor and other civic leaders had a larger vision: combining this with the Orchestra's project, expanding the site already owned by the Orchestra. With the Orchestra's approval, this new plan was implemented.

Two separately conceived concert halls had come together as one grand project. The Philadelphia Orchestra would be the principal tenant in the larger hall, and several highly accomplished local groups would perform in the smaller venue. The beloved Academy of Music, which was undergoing significant renovations, would be home to the Opera Company of Philadelphia and the Pennsylvania Ballet, providing greater access for these companies than previously possible. The Regional Performing Arts Center (RPAC), a private, non-profit body created in September 1996, would administer all three venues.

By this time, another key figure had come on board: Baltimore-born real estate developer Willard G. Rouse III. Rouse had reshaped the city's skyline with his stunning office towers, One and Two Liberty Place, and was instrumental in the completion of the much-admired

CONSTRUCTION SITE, 1999. [PHOTO BY TIM MAIER]

Pennsylvania Convention Center. In 1997 Rouse took over as RPAC Chair, and Stephanie W. Naidoff, an attorney and active civic leader, became President. During her more than four-year tenure, Naidoff brought the project to life, attracting virtually all the necessary funding in record time and laying the groundwork for the organization that would administer the new facilities.

She was succeeded in May 2001 by Leslie Anne Miller, a distinguished Philadelphia lawyer and community activist. Miller, winner of the year 2000 Sandra Day O'Connor Award, the highest recognition given to a female lawyer by the Philadelphia Bar Association, quickly brought about the completion of agreements with the eight artistic companies that reside in The Kimmel Center and the Academy of Music. Continuing to further solidify these working relationships, Miller has also streamlined operations at the Regional Performing Arts Center and responded to staffing needs.

The venture offered many benefits. Philadelphia, the nation's fifth-largest city, was ranked 15th in the number of performance-venue seats. Now it would have greatly increased opportunities to showcase its own native talent, as well as out-of-town performers. Major orchestras and performers from across the country and abroad, who had previously bypassed Philadelphia for lack of an appropriate performance venue, would be eager to perform here, helping the city reaffirm its position as a preeminent center for the arts. The activities of the new center would be varied and inclusive, representing the diversity and cultural richness of the entire region. From all this would come economic growth, increased tourism, and a more dynamic Center City, attracting new hotels, restaurants, and companies, and creating new jobs.

CHOOSING THE TEAM

Twelve architectural firms of international repute were invited to submit proposals. Proposals were also sought for acoustician, theater consultant, and construction manager. After exhaustive review, a team was chosen.

The architect selected was Rafael Viñoly, a native of Uruguay raised in Argentina. As principal of Rafael Viñoly Architects PC, with practices in New York, Tokyo, and Buenos Aires, Viñoly is recognized worldwide for the simplicity and directness of his buildings. As a classically trained pianist, Viñoly is keenly aware of the needs of both performer and audience, and he incorporates this sensitivity into his designs. "Buildings," he has said, "are forms of performance." Among his most acclaimed works is the $1.5 billion Tokyo International Forum, a

seven-acre performing arts complex and convention center that opened in 1996. The *New York Times* described the Forum as "such a perfectly realized building that ... the only thing it can be faulted for is a pursuit of excellence so unyielding that it seems to not quite deserve a place in our world of scintillating compromise."

In the crucial role of acoustician would be Russell Johnson, the Pennsylvania-born founder of the acoustical design firm Artec Consultants, who is credited with revolutionizing the art and science of sound in concert halls. Johnson is responsible for the superb acoustics of the New Jersey Performing Arts Center and the Morton H. Meyerson Symphony Center in Dallas, as well as the internationally applauded concert halls in Birmingham, U.K., and Lucerne, Switzerland. Like Viñoly, he has been honored by his peers, receiving the highest award of the Acoustical Society of America.

As founder of Theatre Projects Consultants, now the preeminent theater consulting organization in the world, Richard Pilbrow has more than 500 projects in 40 countries to his credit. A pioneer of modern stage lighting, he won the Drama Desk and Outer Critic's Circle Awards for best lighting in Harold Prince's Broadway revival of *Showboat*. For The Kimmel Center, he and David Taylor, Principal Consultant in the firm's Connecticut office, oversaw all elements of theater equipment, including lighting, rigging, sightlines, and lifts. Along with Viñoly and Artec, Theatre Projects Consultants conducted numerous interviews and seminars with the Center's potential users, especially the Resident Companies, to ensure that the venues would be shaped to the needs of audiences and performers.

Providing much-needed coordination and continuity in this massive endeavor was the unflappable Project Manager, George Shaeffer, who had been associated with The Philadelphia Orchestra's earlier effort to build its own hall. Shaeffer, a veteran of other major Center City construction projects such as the Gallery at Market East, the Center City Rail Connection, and the Convention Center, would represent RPAC in the day-to-day management of the project.

The team's first task was to determine and research every possible use for the Center. Strengths and weaknesses in performance facilities worldwide were taken into account. Every component of the new

OPPOSITE PAGE: JAMES TRUAX, GLAZIER, WORKS ON THE WEST WALL, JUNE 2001. [PHOTO BY JOHN CARLANO]

INSET: RAFAEL VIÑOLY

The Architect's Touch: Rafael Viñoly

The first orchestra Rafael Viñoly remembers hearing, through his father's record collection, was The Philadelphia Orchestra, under Leopold Stokowski. From this exposure, says the master architect, "I retain an adulation that dates back to childhood."

The opportunity to provide a new home for the Orchestra greatly appealed to Viñoly, but equally important, he says, was the fact that "from the beginning, RPAC's Chair, Willard Rouse, conceived the building as a civic statement." For Viñoly, this idea translates, in the design process, into "accessibility," a quality that—along with grandeur and simplicity—is associated with many of his projects around the world, including the spectacular Tokyo International Forum.

Recognizing the tradition of architectural excellence in Philadelphia, exemplified by major figures such as Frank Furness and Louis Kahn, Viñoly realized early on that the challenge was to create "a landmark for a city of monuments, and at the same time to invite interaction."

"The accessibility we achieved in The Kimmel Center is different from anything I know of," says Viñoly. This is most obvious in Commonwealth Plaza, where "the traditional notion of the lobby is transformed ... The Kimmel Center is a place where you're together with many other people. You see them; there are no barriers." Even the "magic line" that separates performers from audience is minimized in the Center's two halls; Viñoly hopes this will create an environment of trust that invites both better playing and better listening.

"The Kimmel Center forces an interaction between functions that are not necessarily typical of what happens in a performing arts center," says Viñoly. "When you walk around the building, you don't see the complexity ... What occurs is really very dependent upon the performance of the building, of the Orchestra, of RPAC." ∎

construction—from public spaces to a choral warm-up space—
was discussed, with particular focus on the needs of The Philadelphia
Orchestra and the other expected Resident Companies. Finally,
after a year of intense work, the plans were ready to be shared
with the community.

A DREAM UNVEILED

On April 16, 1998, Rafael Viñoly took the stage at the Pennsylvania
Convention Center and faced a rapt audience of about a thousand
civic and cultural leaders, corporate executives, philanthropists, and
the media. All had assembled for the first glimpse of the 429,095-
square-foot building heralded by Mayor Rendell as "the signature
building of this generation of Philadelphians." Mr. Viñoly unveiled
the model. The audience contemplated the design in silence, and
then erupted in applause.

They saw much more than a building. Viñoly had designed a cultural
commons, housed within the space of an entire city block, that subtly
blended indoors and outdoors. A public space where the people of a
diverse city and region could gather, morning and night, in all seasons.
A design that emphasized human interaction, even though it would
incorporate state-of-the-art technology. As for the halls themselves,
they were indeed, as Viñoly himself described them, "two jewels
floating in a transparent box."

The response was overwhelmingly positive. "A wonder of accessible
grandeur," wrote the *Philadelphia Inquirer*. Edmund C. Bacon, the
internationally known city planner responsible for Philadelphia's
remarkable revitalization in the 1950s and 1960s, said the new
building would bring the Avenue together in "a bold and triumphant
musical chord spanning 200 years."

An outpouring of financial support followed, and the building fund
soon crossed the $200 million mark. Prior to the Center's opening,
additional gifts brought the total raised in *The Campaign to Build The
Kimmel Center* close to the full project cost of $255 million plus more
than $10 million in endowment, surpassing the original pre-opening
goal more than six months before the December opening.

THE WORK BEGINS

Groundbreaking took place on November 12, 1998, with Delaware
County's Chester High School Marching Band leading a parade of
bulldozers and other construction equipment from City Hall to the
site, where jackhammers broke ground to fanfares by the brass sections
of The Philadelphia Orchestra and the Concerto Soloists (later
renamed the Chamber Orchestra of Philadelphia).

(continued on page 91)

THE ACOUSTICIAN'S EAR: RUSSELL JOHNSON

FIVE DECADES DEVOTED TO PERFECTING THE ART AND SCIENCE OF ACOUSTICS
HAVE BROUGHT RUSSELL JOHNSON INTERNATIONAL FAME. THE SCORES OF HALLS

FOR WHICH HE HAS PLANNED AND PROVIDED
COMPREHENSIVE ACOUSTICAL SERVICES—
INCLUDING THE MEYERSON SYMPHONY CENTER
IN DALLAS; SYMPHONY HALL IN BIRMINGHAM,
U.K.; AND THE CULTURE AND CONGRESS
CENTER IN LUCERNE, SWITZERLAND—SPEAK TO
HIS DEPTH OF KNOWLEDGE AND STRONG
INSTINCTS ABOUT THIS MYSTERIOUS ENDEAVOR.

"MY MANTRA FOR GREAT SYMPHONY ACOUSTICS, SUCH AS THOSE IN VERIZON
HALL," SAYS JOHNSON, "IS ADJUSTABILITY, VERSATILITY, FLEXIBILITY."

"THE HALL, WHEN COMPLETED," HE EXPLAINS, "MUST BE VERY HOSPITABLE FOR A
LENGTHY LIST OF SERIOUS—AND SOME NOT SO SERIOUS—MUSIC FORMATS."
WHETHER THE PERFORMANCE IS OF A DELICATE NOCTURNE, AS PLAYED BY A SOLO
PIANIST, OR A BLOCKBUSTER SYMPHONIC WORK, THE HALL MUST BE
CAPABLE OF INSTANTLY ADAPTING.

JOHNSON HAD A CLEAR MISSION FROM THE PHILADELPHIA ORCHESTRA,
THE HALL'S MAJOR TENANT. "THEY DID NOT WANT TO CHANGE THE
PHILADELPHIA ORCHESTRA'S FAMOUS SOUND. THEY WANTED A HALL THAT
WOULD SUPPORT THAT SOUND."

INVOLVED FROM THE KIMMEL CENTER'S EARLIEST STAGES OF PLANNING, JOHNSON
BUILT AN ARCHITECTURAL MODEL OF HIS RECOMMENDED ACOUSTICAL DESIGN FOR
VERIZON HALL. "THEN WE HANDED IT OVER TO RAFAEL VIÑOLY," HE RECOLLECTS.
"AND RAFAEL TRANSFORMED THIS BARE-BONES SKELETON INTO HIS MYSTICAL
AND INTRIGUING CONCEPT OF THE AUDITORIUM AS A MUSICAL INSTRUMENT—
IN THIS CASE, A CELLO."

JOHNSON CANNOT SAY ENOUGH ABOUT THE CORE REQUIREMENT OF SILENCE, AND WITH THIS WORD HE REFERS TO MUCH MORE THAN SUBWAY NOISES. HE MEANS THE SOUND OF CONVERSATION IN THE LOBBY, POLICE SIRENS, AIR-CONDITIONING COMPRESSORS, ELEVATORS, ICE-MAKING MACHINES, DRINKING FOUNTAINS. ONCE THIS FOUNDATION OF SILENCE HAS BEEN ACHIEVED, "IT IS THEN POSSIBLE TO CREATE GLORIOUS SOUND."

PERELMAN THEATER IMPOSED A DIFFERENT AND EQUALLY CHALLENGING SET OF ACOUSTICAL REQUIREMENTS: THOSE OF DRAMA, DANCE, POP MUSIC, SEMINARS, RECITALS, CHAMBER MUSIC, AND MUSICAL COMEDY. ONCE AGAIN, JOHNSON'S PHILOSOPHY OF FLEXIBILITY RESULTED IN A HALL ATTUNED TO THE NEEDS OF EACH MEDIUM.

RUSSELL JOHNSON'S WORK AT THE KIMMEL CENTER DOES NOT END WITH THE OPENING. HIS FINELY TUNED EARS WILL BE LISTENING CAREFULLY TO DETERMINE WHAT REFINEMENTS MIGHT STILL BE MADE.

THE DESIGNER'S EYE: RICHARD PILBROW

ALONG WITH ARCHITECTURAL AND ACOUSTICAL EXPERTISE, THEATER DESIGN IS A CRUCIAL ELEMENT IN THE DEVELOPMENT OF A SUPERIOR PERFORMING

ARTS VENUE. IN THIS AREA, RICHARD PILBROW, FOUNDER AND CHAIR OF THE ESTEEMED LONDON FIRM THEATRE PROJECTS CONSULTANTS, BRINGS DECADES OF EXPERIENCE AND KNOWLEDGE TO THE KIMMEL CENTER TEAM.

HAVING BECOME ACQUAINTED WITH PHILADELPHIA THROUGH HIS WORK AS A LIGHTING DESIGNER AT THE SHUBERT THEATER, PILBROW SAYS THAT, WHEN INTRODUCED TO THE PROJECT, HE WAS "IMPRESSED WITH THE VISION OF

BILL ROUSE, WHICH SUPPORTED MAYOR RENDELL'S CONCEPT OF THE AVENUE OF THE ARTS AND THE 'REBIRTH' OF DOWNTOWN PHILADELPHIA."

WORKING IN CLOSE COLLABORATION WITH RAFAEL VIÑOLY AND RUSSELL JOHNSON, AND IN CONSULTATION WITH RPAC'S RESIDENT COMPANIES, THEATRE PROJECTS WAS RESPONSIBLE FOR WHAT PILBROW REFERS TO AS "THE FINAL SPACE PROGRAM OF THE WHOLE KIMMEL CENTER." SPECIFICALLY, THIS INVOLVED THE CONCEPT DESIGN OF VERIZON HALL AND PERELMAN THEATER, AS WELL AS THE OVERALL PLANNING OF THE BUILDING. FROM SEATING AND SIGHTLINES TO PERFORMANCE EQUIPMENT, FROM ELEVATORS TO MOVING CANOPIES AND ABSORPTION DEVICES, THE FIRM ENSURED THAT THE FINEST IN SIGHT AND SOUND WOULD BE ACHIEVED.

PILBROW SAYS THAT A MAJOR CHALLENGE IN VERIZON HALL WAS TO "DESIGN A CONCERT HALL WHERE THE STAGE HAS THE FLEXIBILITY TO ALLOW FOR OTHER EVENTS WITHOUT ANY COMPROMISE TO THE CENTRAL ROLE OF PRESENTING SYMPHONIC MUSIC." HE ALSO TOOK INTO SERIOUS ACCOUNT THE MORE "THEATRICAL" STYLES OF PRESENTATION BEING INVESTIGATED TODAY IN THE CONCERT HALL, THROUGH SOPHISTICATED STAGE LIGHTING AND PROJECTION EQUIPMENT.

PERELMAN THEATER POSED UNIQUE CHALLENGES. IT WOULD HAVE TO CHANGE RAPIDLY FROM A CHAMBER MUSIC VENUE TO A SMALL THEATER, AT MINIMUM OPERATING COST. THE DESIGN DEVELOPED BY HIS FIRM, SAYS PILBROW, WAS AN "EXCEPTIONALLY INTIMATE 'COURTYARD THEATER' WITH THE AUDIENCE ON THREE LEVELS WRAPPING AROUND A CENTRAL FLEXIBLE SPACE."

DAVID TAYLOR, PILBROW'S ASSOCIATE, ADDS: "WE WANTED SPECIFICALLY TO CREATE A VENUE THAT WOULD BE RESPONSIVE TO THE NEEDS OF THE CITY, ITS ARTS CONSTITUENTS AND ITS AUDIENCES—ALL THOSE WHO WOULD MAKE THE KIMMEL CENTER THEIR HOME. THEY, IN EFFECT, OWN IT, AND WE BELIEVE THEY WILL LOVE IT." ∎

TOP: MAYOR ED RENDELL AT THE BUILDING DESIGN
UNVEILING, APRIL 16, 1998.

MIDDLE: RPAC CHAIR WILLARD G. ROUSE III AND
PRESIDENT STEPHANIE W. NAIDOFF (LEFT) WITH
CAROLINE AND SIDNEY KIMMEL AT THE SECOND ANNUAL
FOUNDERS' DAY DINNER, JUNE 14, 2000.
[PHOTO BY KELLY & MASSA]

BOTTOM: RUTH AND RAYMOND PERELMAN, SECOND
ANNUAL FOUNDERS' DAY DINNER. [PHOTO BY
KELLY & MASSA]

RIGHT: PHOTO BY JOHN CARLANO

A major acoustic concern was protecting the venues against vibrations from the Broad Street subway, so that ideal sound conditions could be achieved for live and recorded performance. In one of many innovative moves, Artec found the answer in 331 vibration pads—each eight inches thick, made of compressed rubber and steel, similar to those used for buildings in earthquake-prone areas. Each of the performance spaces would be constructed as a freestanding building within the Center, resting on the vibration pads.

By May 1999, 135,000 cubic yards of earth had been removed from the 2.3-acre site, and pouring of the walls and foundations began. Each hall would be surrounded by two walls of filled concrete block to prevent outside ambient noise from entering the performance spaces. By the time the Center was completed, enough concrete had been poured to build a sidewalk from Philadelphia to Harrisburg.

CITY COUNCIL PRESIDENT (AND FUTURE MAYOR) JOHN F. STREET ADDRESSES THE SECOND ANNUAL FOUNDERS' DAY DINNER. [PHOTO BY KELLY & MASSA]

In July 1999, Pennsylvania Governor Tom Ridge transferred to RPAC the $8 million the previous administration had promised the project, and he added a major vote of confidence: an additional $20 million. With the $35 million grant made to the original Philadelphia Orchestra hall project, this brought the Commonwealth's total contribution to an unprecedented $63 million. Ridge visited the construction site on July 8, 1999, to announce the new pledge. While a brass quintet played, a giant check was lifted by crane from the bottom of the excavation and brought to the Governor for his signature. In recognition of this remarkable gift, the Center's magnificent atrium, which houses the performance venues and all amenities, is named Commonwealth Plaza.

In addition to the Commonwealth's support, the City of Philadelphia, under the leadership of Mayor Rendell and then City Council President (now Mayor) John F. Street, granted $30 million to The Kimmel Center's Capital Program. Thus, governmental support for the project exceeded $93 million; the rest of the funds were raised within the community.

Gradually, the project moved forward. Once the steel superstructure had been completed, it was time to erect the elegant glass-vaulted roof that gives the building its distinctive shape. As the 14-foot-long pieces of glass, each weighing 1,044 pounds, were delivered and maneuvered into place, a dramatic high-wire act ensued, with sections hoisted by crane to workers stationed on a movable triangular scaffold. (This scaffold will be used to clean the outside of the glass skylight once the building is opened.)

Through it all, the project's Construction Manager, L.F. Driscoll Company/Artis T. Ore, watched weather conditions anxiously, while in the nearby RPAC offices a sign was posted with a daily countdown: "365 Days: Grand Opening." As the countdown continued, the excitement was palpable. At times, as many as 450 workers were on-site: cement masons, bricklayers, rod setters, glaziers, engineers, ironworkers, plumbers, painters, and electricians—the courageous heroes of this ambitious undertaking. On Valentine's Day, 2001, RPAC said "Thank you!" with an on-site breakfast for the crew. The gratitude continued throughout the year for an amazing job well done. In early July 2001, the building was "topped off," as the last piece of steel was hoisted into place. Soon, the glass roof was completed and

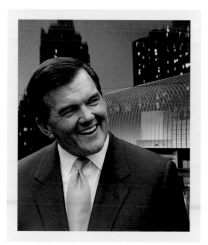

GOV. TOM RIDGE VISITS THE CONSTRUCTION SITE, JULY 8, 1999.

interior work—flooring, painting, finish carpentry, and carpeting—could be carried forward without concern about rain.

It had been a long and exciting show, different from those that would soon occur on the Center's stages, but the performers on the scaffolds and the audiences on the street would remember it for years to come. And, in an odd sort of way, so would the building. RPAC Chair Rouse, speaking at a New York press conference on the progress of the construction, made this telling comment: "The public relishes the building, and the building relishes them."

THE KIMMEL CENTER UP CLOSE

Within its soaring Commonwealth Plaza, The Kimmel Center features two major performance venues, a black-box theater, a choral room, and an education center, as well as many ancillary spaces.

Verizon Hall is the focal point of the Center, named in recognition of a $14.5 million contribution from the philanthropic arm of Verizon Communications (formerly Bell Atlantic), continuing its long history of support for the arts. Despite the hall's 2,500 seats and nearly 100-foot height, it has a feeling of warmth and intimacy. So strong are the musical allusions within this venue that audiences might imagine themselves inside a vast, masterfully calibrated musical instrument. The ceilings and walls are covered in rich mahogany similar to that used in the finest stringed instruments. The side balconies gently curve inward at the center, giving the hall its characteristic cello shape. The shape is both aesthetically pleasing and contributes to optimal acoustics and sightlines. It also allows for a rare feature: seating behind the orchestra that faces the conductor, giving audience members seated there a "musician's-eye view" of the performance.

The science and art of acoustics, as practiced by Artec, reach a high point in this state-of-the-art venue. The hall is noteworthy for the three-piece, fully adjustable canopy that hovers above the stage, and for floor-to-ceiling reverberation chambers on both sides. The chambers are located behind panels that open and close to accommodate the changing acoustical needs of a solo pianist, a string quartet, a baroque chamber piece, or a symphony with massive orchestral forces.

The resulting sound is resonant, clear, full, and warm, with the unique tone of each instrument faithfully maintained. Thanks to the construction and dimensions at the front end of the hall, musicians will hear themselves accurately, a vital feature frequently missing from concert halls. Silence is another crucial, but sometimes overlooked, ingredient of the hall's acoustics. According to Russell Johnson, "Silence is ... the unique, magical foundation for the other acoustic attributes—complete freedom from noise." Together, all these acoustic features will facilitate recording, filming, telecasting—and listening.

Perelman Theater is named for Philadelphians Ruth and Raymond G. Perelman, who early on showed their faith in the project with a gift of $5 million. This venue is as unique for small-scale performances as Verizon is for large ones. It features a rotating stage, 75 feet in

ARCHITECT RAFAEL VIÑOLY AT THE SECOND ANNUAL FOUNDERS' DAY DINNER, JUNE 14, 2000. [PHOTO BY KELLY & MASSA]

diameter, which can transform the space from a recital hall with a fixed shell to a proscenium theater, complete with fly-loft for storing sets. No need for stagehands to laboriously change the configuration, for the stage is motorized and remote-controlled by a single unit.

Floor-level seating can be lowered by elevator to the basement and retracted, allowing for many types of entertainment: cabaret, ballroom dancing, and experimental performances. The upper balcony can be closed, transforming a venue with 650 seats to one with 250. Another welcome feature is the flexible, springy floor with a depth of stage of 40 feet, ideal for dance companies. As in Verizon Hall, the acoustics can be adjusted to suit the performers. Perelman Theater has been specifically designed with the differing needs of RPAC's Resident Companies in mind.

From its inception, the Regional Performing Arts Center has been committed to arts education. A generous $3.5 million grant from the pharmaceutical firm Merck and Company has made possible the Merck Arts Education Center. Designed to complement the education programs of the Resident Companies, the Center will be open to visitors of all ages and will host an array of arts education programs and events. An interactive, user-friendly space, the Merck Center will adapt emerging technology and utilize local artistic talent for educational purposes. For example, visitors might take part in a sing-along, play a digital drum set, "scratch" a record over a hip-hop beat, join in a theater workshop, take a dance master class, or sit in on a meet-the-artist session prior to a performance. A distance-learning program will provide resources to teachers and students in Philadelphia and the surrounding region, as well as to senior citizens and special-needs individuals.

Another flexible performance space is the Innovation Studio, located one level below the lobby. A 2,500-square-foot space, akin to a black-box theater, the Studio seats up to 150 and is suitable for experimental theater and, with its ballet barres and wall mirrors, dance. It is an ideal setting for growing organizations in need of rehearsal and performance space, and for a wide range of productions that will give meaning to its name.

The Rendell Room, a choral room, is named in honor of Philadelphia's former first couple, Edward G. and Marjorie O. Rendell, whose commitment helped bring The Kimmel Center to fruition.

Other public facilities within the complex include the 200-seat restaurant, with international cuisine prepared by the award-winning Restaurant Associates. Comcast Circle, the Center's exquisite entertainment suite, will be a distinctive address for private dinners, receptions, and other business and social events. The Rooftop Garden, shaded by 16 trees, provides an oasis of green on the Philadelphia skyline, a stopping-off place for afternoon tea, evening cocktails, or post-concert conversation. The Center also features amenities such as a musicians' lounge, artist reception rooms, dressing rooms, a music library, offices for arts administrators, and underground parking.

Into the Future

There are no limits to what innovations might take place at The Kimmel Center over the decades, given its highly versatile spaces and its advanced technologies.

In the classic 1940 film *Fantasia*, the technological wizardry of Walt Disney Studios combined with the musical genius of Leopold Stokowski and The Philadelphia Orchestra to create a seamless and accessible blend of classical music and animation. Before we know it, Kimmel Center audiences may listen to and *see* great music, thanks to any number of emerging computer technologies that translate a composer's score into dancing, three-dimensional color. And in the Merck Arts Education Center, technology will help foster the performers and audiences of the future. Here, children working in groups might design and build their own stage sets, try out costume ideas, and even compose their own operas, all with the aid of an interactive computer program.

And that's just the beginning. ∎

PHOTO BY JOHN CARLANO

A Salute to the Hardhats

A few of the more than 2,000 construction workers whose dedication and efforts made The Kimmel Center possible. Left to right: Chris Colbridge, carpenter, Philadelphia Duggan & Marcon; John Fabry, steamfitter, Herman Goldner Co.; Billy Warne, sheet metal worker, SSM Industries; William Scott (a.k.a. "Footloose"), electrician, Williard, Inc.; Beth Galdo, assistant superintendent, L.F. Driscoll Co.; Ron Wahl, carpenter, Philadelphia Duggan & Marcon; Keryatta Bundy, carpenter/stud driller, Philadelphia Duggan & Marcon. [Photos by John Carlano]

THE ACADEMY OF MUSIC

The Grand Old Lady of Locust Street

TOP: THE ACADEMY'S BROAD STREET ENTRANCE. [PHOTO BY PETER OLSEN]

BOTTOM: AN 1857 *HARPER'S WEEKLY* ENGRAVING OF THE NEWLY OPENED ACADEMY. [PHOTO COURTESY OF THE PHILADELPIHA ORCHESTRA ASSOCIATION ARCHIVES]

January 20, 1857, arrived with more than a flurry of excitement on Locust Street—it was, in fact, a blizzard. What was intended to be a festive opening of the most exciting new opera house in the United States was foiled by the weather—a snowstorm accompanied by subzero temperatures and fierce winds.

Six days later, on January 26, Philadelphia's Academy of Music finally opened with a Grand Ball and Promenade Concert. On that evening, hundreds of carriages lined Broad Street, discharging ladies in sable coats and gowns of lace or silk, some of which had long trains. Accompanying them were gentlemen in top hats, tails, and patent-leather shoes. Thousands of spectators gathered outside to glimpse the posh concertgoers and the impressive new building.

The somewhat austere brick-and-brownstone exterior of the 130,000-square-foot Academy of Music gave no hint of what patrons would find within. Neo-baroque in style, the interior featured a curved auditorium, three tiers stacked above the main floor, which seated 2,900 patrons; wide corridors; richly adorned stairways; and a ballroom with glass doors (later replaced with mirrors) overlooking Broad Street. The seats were covered with crimson velvet and the walls with ornate crimson wallpaper. The woodwork was white and gold. A bas-relief bust of Mozart crowned the proscenium arch, above which, on the left, was the seated figure of Poetry and, to the right, that of Music. Exquisitely carved and gilded wood sculptural decorations adorned the hall, and ceiling murals depicted allegorical figures.

Most eye-catching of all was the huge crystal chandelier—50 feet in circumference, 16 feet in diameter, and weighing 5,000 pounds—suspended from the center of the dome. Despite its size, the chandelier seemed a light, airy creation, its hundreds of glittering lights casting a magical glow over the hall.

The creators of this 19th-century wonder were a pair of local architects, Napoleon Le Brun and Gustav Runge, whose design, based on Milan's La Scala, had won the competition for the project in 1854. The cornerstone was laid in July 1855, and by December all that remained was the addition of the roof.

Le Brun and Runge paid particular attention to sightlines and acoustics. Their design featured an open horseshoe shape that offered greater visibility from the balconies than most opera

houses of the time. A three-foot-thick brick wall, the inner sides of which were lined with studding and pine boards to absorb sound and prevent echoes, enclosed the auditorium. Walls were kept soft to cushion the sound, and resonance pits were placed under the auditorium floor and stage.

The Academy of Music soon became the focus of Philadelphia's musical and social life, and assumed a central place among the nation's opera houses. Giuseppe Verdi's *Il trovatore* was presented in the Academy's opening year—just five years after its first performance. The Academy hosted the American premieres of other major works in the operatic canon, including Charles Gounod's *Faust* and Richard Wagner's *Der fliegende Holländer.* In April 1884, the new Metropolitan Opera gave its first performance at the Academy, Giacomo Meyerbeer's *Les Huguenots*; this was the beginning of a long and brilliant association, with the Met's most famous singers coming to Philadelphia season after season.

Indeed, the roster of renowned artists—vocal, instrumental, dance, and theatrical—who have performed at the Academy of Music is a "Who's Who in the Performing Arts": Marian Anderson, Vladimir Horowitz, Anna Pavlova, Enrico Caruso, Itzhak Perlman, Edwin Forrest, Nellie Melba, Margot Fonteyn, Rudolf Nureyev, Luciano Pavarotti, Isaac Stern, Leontyne Price, and Arthur Rubinstein, just to name a few.

The world's great composers also have come to the Academy, sometimes to hear their music performed, and sometimes to conduct it. The first was Pyotr Ilyich Tchaikovsky in 1891, followed by Gustav Mahler, Sergei Rachmaninoff, Richard Strauss, Camille Saint-Saëns, Igor Stravinsky, Aaron Copland, and John Adams. Giacomo Puccini attended a performance of his *Madama Butterfly*, with leading roles sung by Caruso and the brilliant soprano Geraldine Farrar.

The Academy has been linked with The Philadelphia Orchestra since that great ensemble was founded in 1900. Under the direction of its distinguished leaders—Fritz Scheel, Carl Pohlig, Leopold Stokowski, Eugene Ormandy, Riccardo Muti, and Wolfgang Sawallisch—the Orchestra's evolving roster of one-hundred-plus outstanding musicians has presented a century of inspired performances.

Maestro Sawallisch has the richly deserved honor of ushering the orchestra he has led for almost a decade from this grand and beloved old home to The Kimmel Center for the Performing Arts, inaugurating a new century of music in a new home.

Over the years, the Academy has hosted far more than music. Numerous presidents have visited, including Ulysses S. Grant, who was nominated for his second term here. President Grover Cleveland attended the centennial celebration of the U.S. Constitution at the Academy. And, in 1889, the first indoor football game in Philadelphia—between the University of Pennsylvania and the Riverton Club of Princeton—took place on a specially installed wooden floor placed over the Academy's parquet seats.

Even the basement has a rich history. When the building opened, the basement housed an elegant restaurant with drawing rooms off the main areas where patrons sipped sherry and smoked cigars. During World War II, the restaurant was converted into a "Stage Door Canteen," serving refreshments to men and women from the Armed Forces and entertaining them with guest appearances by such stars as Duke Ellington, Frank Sinatra, and Gertrude Lawrence. Between 1942 and 1945, the Canteen hosted more than one million servicemen and women.

As the Academy of Music approached its 1957 centennial, the hall was beginning to show its age. To raise funds for needed improvements, The Philadelphia Orchestra Association, which purchased the Academy in the mid-1950s, established the Restoration Fund Office. The centennial year saw the inauguration of the annual Academy of Music Anniversary Concert & Ball. Always held on the fourth Saturday of January, the Ball will remain at the Academy, even when the Orchestra settles into its Verizon Hall home. With internationally recognized performers (including singers Birgit Nilsson and Maria Callas, pianist Van Cliburn, flutist James Galway, and comedian Harpo Marx), the Academy Ball has been the highlight of the Philadelphia social season, and one of the most successful ventures of its kind nationally. Proceeds support the Academy restoration and The Philadelphia Orchestra Association.

The Academy Concert and Ball has funded many restoration projects, including purchase of a new main house curtain, conservation of ceiling murals and wood sculptures, restoration of the main lobby and grand staircase, and renovation of the ballroom. Two new elevators were installed, thanks to the generosity of Ambassador and Mrs. Walter H. Annenberg, making all levels accessible to every patron.

With its goal set at $30 million, the Project for the 21st Century was launched in 1994. This six-phase project involves major structural and acoustical improvements, backstage theatrical modernization, and improvements in patron services. Remarkably, this work has not interfered with scheduled performances. A complete overhaul of the stage and backstage area resulted in a state-of-the-art sound and lighting system, and more improvements are scheduled. A final phase of work, scheduled for completion in summer 2002, will raise the roof over the stage and install a new rigging system, allowing for better manipulation of scenery and lighting equipment.

Today, the Academy of Music is the oldest continuously operating opera house in the nation and one of the busiest performance venues in the world. As a new century begins, the Grand Old Lady of Locust Street has a new partner: The Kimmel Center for the Performing Arts. Together, the majestic and traditional Academy and the strikingly modern Kimmel Center form a perfect union—namely, the Regional Performing Arts Center, one of the largest and most important complexes of its kind in the nation. Boasting 21st-century technology, the 19th-century Academy will be home to the Opera Company of Philadelphia and Pennsylvania Ballet. It will also host Broadway shows, major stars, and touring groups, many of whom previously bypassed Philadelphia for lack of an appropriate venue. Today, as ever, the Lady beckons. ■

A POSTER OUTSIDE THE ACADEMY ADVERTISES AN APPEARANCE BY RUSSIAN PIANIST AND COMPOSER SERGEI RACHMANINOFF. [PHOTO COURTESY OF THE PHILADELPIHA ORCHESTRA ASSOCIATION ARCHIVES]

The Regional Performing Arts Center Inaugural Season

Fri., Jan. 4, 8 P.M.
Bill Cosby
Verizon Hall

Sun., Jan. 6, 7:30 P.M.
**Jerry Blavat's "Legends of
Rock 'n' Roll"**
Verizon Hall

Wed., Jan. 16, 8 P.M.
Israel Philharmonic Orchestra
Zubin Mehta, conductor
BARTÓK *The Miraculous
    Mandarin: Suite*
R. STRAUSS *Ein Heldenleben*, Op. 40
Verizon Hall

Thu., Jan. 17, 7:30 P.M.
Fri., Jan. 18, 7:30 P.M.
Sat., Jan. 19, 2:30 P.M., 7:30 P.M.
**PHILADANCO
Martin Luther King Jr. Tribute**
Perelman Theater

Sun., Jan. 27, 2:30 P.M.
**Christian Tetzlaff, violin
Leif Ove Andsnes, piano**
BEETHOVEN Sonata, Op. 30 No. 2
    in C minor
SCHUBERT Duo in A minor
BARTÓK Sonata No. 1
Perelman Theater

Fri., Feb. 1, 8 P.M.
Three Mo' Tenors
Victor Trent Cook
Rodrick Dixon
Thomas Young
Verizon Hall

Sun., Feb. 3, 2 P.M.
André Watts, piano
MUSSORGSKY *Pictures at an
    Exhibition*, plus other works
    to be announced
Verizon Hall

Thu., Feb. 7, 8 P.M.
**Royal Concertgebouw Orchestra
Amsterdam**
Riccardo Chailly, conductor
Janice Watson, soprano
Petra Lang, alto
Westminster Symphonic Choir
MAHLER Symphony No. 2 in C minor
    (Resurrection)
Verizon Hall

Sun., Feb. 17, 2 P.M.
Renée Fleming, soprano
Steven Blier, piano
Philadelphia Recital Debut
Verizon Hall

Fri., Mar. 1, 8 P.M.
**Keith Jarrett, piano
Gary Peacock, bass
Jack DeJohnette, drums**
First Philadelphia Performance
    in 20 Years
Verizon Hall

Mon., Mar. 4, 8 P.M.
Moiseyev Dance Company
Verizon Hall

Fri., Mar. 8, 8 P.M.
James Galway, flute
Phillip Moll, piano
Verizon Hall

Fri., Mar. 8, 7:30 P.M.
Sat., Mar. 9, 7:30 P.M.
Sun., Mar. 10, 2:30 P.M.
Mark Morris Dance Group
Perelman Theater

Sun., Mar. 10, 2 P.M.
The Chieftains
Verizon Hall

Fri., Mar. 15, 7:30 P.M.
**Anne Sofie von Otter,
mezzo-soprano**
Bengt Forsberg, piano
Philadelphia Recital Debut
Perelman Theater

Sun., Mar. 24, 2 P.M.
Sweet Honey in the Rock
Verizon Hall

Fri., Mar. 29, 8 P.M.
**Herbie Hancock
Dianne Reeves**
Verizon Hall

Fri., April 5, 8 P.M.
**Lincoln Center Jazz Orchestra
with Wynton Marsalis, Conductor**
Verizon Hall

Sun., April 7, 7:30 P.M.
Bobby McFerrin
Solo acoustic concert
Verizon Hall

Fri., April 12, 8 P.M.
Boston Symphony Orchestra
Seiji Ozawa, conductor
BARTÓK Concerto,
    Two Pianos and Percussion
BERLIOZ *Symphonie fantastique*,
    Op. 14
Verizon Hall

Fri., April 12, 7:30 P.M.
Sat., April 13, 7:30 P.M.
Sun., April 14, 2:30 P.M.
Bill T. Jones: *The Breathing Show*
Perelman Theater

Sun., April 14, 7:30 P.M.
**Emerson String Quartet
Kalichstein-Laredo-Robinson Trio**
A Joint 25th Anniversary Concert
BEETHOVEN Trio (Allegretto)
    WOO 39, in B-flat
WOLF *Italian Serenade*
SCHOENBERG *Verklärte Nacht*, Op. 4
BRAHMS Piano Quartet, Op. 25
    in G minor
Perelman Theater

Sun., April 21, 7:30 P.M.
The Buena Vista Social Club presents
Omara Portuondo
Philadelphia Solo Debut
Verizon Hall

Thu., April 25, 8 P.M.
Fri., April 26, 8 P.M.
Sat., April 27, 2 P.M., 8 P.M.
Sun., April 28, 2 P.M.
Alvin Ailey American Dance Theater
Academy of Music

Sun., April 28, 2 P.M.
Itzhak Perlman, violin
Rohan De Silva, piano
Verizon Hall

Thu., May 16, 7:30 P.M.
Fri., May 17, 7:30 P.M.
Sat., May 18, 2:30 P.M., 7:30 P.M.
The Reduced Shakespeare Company
*The Complete Works of William
    Shakespeare (Abridged)*
Philadelphia Debut
Perelman Theater

Fri., May 17, 8 P.M.
New York Philharmonic
Kurt Masur, conductor
BERNSTEIN Serenade
MAHLER Symphony No. 1 in D Major
    (Titan)
Verizon Hall

Wed., May 22, 7:30 P.M.
John Williams, guitar
Philadelphia Recital Debut
Perelman Theater

*For tickets, call Ticket Philadelphia at
215-893-1999, visit the Box Office
at The Kimmel Center, or visit
www.kimmelcenter.org.*

THE PHILADELPHIA ORCHESTRA

Thu., Jan. 3, 8 P.M.
Fri., Jan. 4, 2 P.M.
Sat., Jan. 5, 8 P.M.
Tue., Jan. 8, 8 P.M.
Wolfgang Sawallisch, conductor
KERNIS *Color Wheel*
RAVEL *Daphnis et Chloé,* Suite No. 2
SIBELIUS Symphony No. 2
Verizon Hall

Sat., Jan. 5, 11:30 A.M.
Family Concert:
The Thrill of the Orchestra
Wolfgang Sawallisch, conductor
Jonah Kim, cello (2001 Greenfield
    Student Competition Winner)
Charlotte Blake Alston, host and
    narrator
Verizon Hall

Wed., Jan. 9, 8 P.M.
Martin Luther King Jr.
Tribute Concert
Raymond Harvey, conductor

Fri., Jan. 11, 8 P.M.
Sat., Jan. 12, 8 P.M.
Wolfgang Sawallisch, conductor
Murray Perahia, piano
BEETHOVEN Overture to
    The Creatures of Prometheus
BEETHOVEN Piano Concerto No. 1
BEETHOVEN Piano Concerto No. 3
Verizon Hall

Sun., Jan. 13, 3 P.M.
Chamber Music Concert
Members of The Philadelphia
    Orchestra
Wolfgang Sawallisch, piano
BEETHOVEN Piano Sonata No. 28,
    Op. 101 (arranged for string
    quartet)
BEETHOVEN Quintet, Op. 16
    (for piano and winds)
BEETHOVEN Septet, Op. 20
Perelman Theater

Tue., Jan. 15, 8 P.M.
Thu., Jan. 17, 8 P.M.
Wolfgang Sawallisch, conductor
Murray Perahia, piano
BEETHOVEN *Coriolan* Overture
BEETHOVEN Piano Concerto No. 2
BEETHOVEN Piano Concerto No. 4
Verizon Hall

Fri., Jan. 18, 2 P.M.
Sat., Jan. 19, 8 P.M.
Wolfgang Sawallisch, conductor
Murray Perahia, piano
BEETHOVEN Overture to *Egmont*
BEETHOVEN Symphony No. 8
BEETHOVEN Piano Concerto No. 5
    ("Emperor")
Verizon Hall

Thu., Jan. 24, 8 P.M.
Fri., Jan. 25, 2 P.M.
Tue., Jan. 29, 8 P.M.
Wolfgang Sawallisch, conductor
Roberto Díaz, viola
LISZT Prometheus
    (Symphonic Poem No. 5)
HINDEMITH *Der Schwanendreher*
    (Concerto for Viola and
    Small Orchestra)
DVORÁK Symphony No. 7
Verizon Hall

Sat., Jan. 26, 7:30 P.M.
Academy of Music 145th Anniversary
Concert and Ball
Wolfgang Sawallisch, conductor
Heidi Grant Murphy, soprano
Joshua Bell, violin
Academy of Music

Thu., Jan. 31, 8 P.M.
Fri., Feb. 1, 2 P.M.
Sat., Feb. 2, 8 P.M.
Sir Roger Norrington, conductor
BEETHOVEN Symphony No. 2
BERLIOZ Symphonie fantastique
Verizon Hall

Sat., Feb. 2, 10 A.M., 11:15 A.M.,
    12:30 P.M.
Mon., Feb. 4, 10 A.M., 11:15 A.M.
Sound-All-Around
(for children ages 3–5)
Academy of Music Ballroom

Tue., Feb. 5, 8 P.M.
Wed., Feb. 6, 8 P.M.
Fri., Feb. 8, 2 P.M.
Sat., Feb. 9, 8 P.M.
Christoph Eschenbach, conductor
ROUSE Symphony No. 2
DVORÁK Symphony No. 9 ("From
    the New World")
Verizon Hall

Wed., Feb. 13, 8 P.M.
Fri., Feb. 15, 2 P.M.
Sat., Feb. 16, 8 P.M.
Neeme Järvi, conductor
Thomas Zehetmair, violin
MOZART Violin Concerto
    No. 4, K. 218
GLIÈRE Symphony No. 3
    ("Ilya Muromets")
Verizon Hall

Thu., Feb. 14, 8 P.M.
Valentine's Concert
Rossen Milanov, conductor
Verizon Hall

Sun., Feb. 17, 3 P.M.
Chamber Music Concert
Members of The Philadelphia
    Orchestra
BRIDGE Trio Rhapsody
    (for two violins and viola)
RAVEL Piano Trio
BRAHMS String Quartet No. 3,
    Op. 67
Perelman Theater

Mon., Feb. 18, 7 P.M.
Access Concert:
"Schubert Unfinished"
Robert Kapilow, conductor
    and host
Verizon Hall

Thu., Feb. 21, 8 P.M.
Fri., Feb. 22, 2 P.M.
Sat., Feb. 23, 8 P.M.
Roberto Abbado, conductor
Vadim Repin, violin
PROKOFIEV Overture on
    Hebrew Themes
TCHAIKOVSKY Violin Concerto
BRAHMS Symphony No. 1
Verizon Hall

Thu., Feb. 28, 8 P.M.
Fri., Mar. 1, 2 P.M.
Sat., Mar. 2, 8 P.M.
Roberto Abbado, conductor
Katia Labèque, piano
Marielle Labèque, piano
RAVEL Suite from *Mother Goose*
BERIO Concerto for Two Pianos
    and Orchestra
BARTÓK Concerto for Orchestra
Verizon Hall

Thu., Mar. 7, 8 P.M.
Fri., Mar. 8, 2 P.M.
Sat., Mar. 9, 8 P.M.
Tue., Mar. 12, 8 P.M.
Sir Simon Rattle, conductor
Dawn Upshaw, soprano
STRAUSS Voices of Spring Waltz
SCHOENBERG String Quartet No. 2,
    for string orchestra and soprano
SCHUBERT Symphony in C major
    ("The Great")
Verizon Hall

Thu., Mar. 14, 8 P.M.
Fri., Mar. 15, 8 P.M.
Sat., Mar. 16, 8 P.M.
Sir Simon Rattle, conductor
H. K. Gruber, chansonnier
GRUBER *Frankenstein!!*
MAHLER Symphony No. 5
Verizon Hall

Sun., Mar. 17, 3 P.M.
Chamber Music Concert
Members of The Philadelphia
    Orchestra
MAHLER Quartet for piano
    and strings
BERG String Quartet
SCHOENBERG Selections
    from *Cabaret Songs*
EISLER Selections from
    Newspaper Clippings
KREISLER String Quartet
Perelman Theater

Thu., Mar. 21, 8 P.M.
Fri., Mar. 22, 8 P.M.
Sat., Mar. 23, 8 P.M.
Sir Simon Rattle, conductor
Pinchas Zukerman, violin
BERG Violin Concerto
BRUCKNER Symphony No. 9
Verizon Hall

Thu., April 4, 8 P.M.
Fri., April 5, 2 P.M.
Sat., April 6, 8 P.M.
Charles Dutoit, conductor
Martha Argerich, piano
BERLIOZ Rob Roy Overture
CHOPIN Piano Concerto No. 1
STRAVINSKY *Petrushka*
    (original version, 1911)
Verizon Hall

Sat., April 6, 11:30 A.M.
**Family Concert: "And
Furthermore They Bite"**
Robert Kapilow, conductor
Verizon Hall

Thu., April 11, 8 P.M.
Fri., April 12, 2 P.M.
Sat., April 13, 8 P.M.
Tue., April 16, 8 P.M.
James Conlon, conductor
Linda Watson, soprano
BEETHOVEN Symphony No. 1
WAGNER Excerpts from
    Götterdämmerung
Verizon Hall

Thu., April 18, 8 P.M.
Fri., April 19, 8 P.M.
Sat., April 20, 8 P.M.
Sir Andrew Davis, conductor
The Hilliard Ensemble
The Philadelphia Singers Chorale
    (David Hayes, music director)
The American Boychoir (Vincent
    Metallo, music director)
VAUGHAN WILLIAMS Symphony
    No. 5
MacMILLAN *Quickening*
Verizon Hall

Sat., April 20, 10 A.M., 11:15 A.M.,
    12:30 P.M.
Mon., April 22, 10 A.M., 11:15 A.M.
**Sound-All-Around
(for children ages 3–5)**
Academy of Music Ballroom

Sun., April 21, 3 P.M.
Chamber Music Concert
Members of The Philadelphia
    Orchestra
Gary Graffman, piano
BRAHMS Piano Trio Op. 114
BRITTEN String Quartet No. 2
KORNGOLD Suite Op. 23 (for piano
    lefthand and strings)
Perelman Theater

Tue., April 23, 7 P.M.
Access Concert: "Rhapsody in Blue"
William Eddins, conductor
Verizon Hall

Thu., April 25, 8 P.M.
Fri., April 26, 8 P.M.
Sat., April 27, 8 P.M.
Roberto Abbado, conductor
Gil Shaham, violin
Orli Shaham, piano
MENDELSSOHN Hebrides Overture
    ("Fingal's Cave")
MENDELSSOHN Concerto in D
    minor for Violin, Piano,
    and String Orchestra
RACHMANINOFF Symphony No. 3
Verizon Hall

Sat., May 4, 11:30 A.M.
**Family Concert:
"Beethoven Lives Upstairs"**
Luis Biava, conductor
with Classical Kids
Verizon Hall

Fri., May 10, 8 P.M.
Sat., May 11, 8 P.M.
Tue., May 14, 8 P.M.
Wolfgang Sawallisch, conductor
Emanuel Ax, piano
PENDERECKI Piano Concerto
BRAHMS Symphony No. 3
Verizon Hall

Thu., May 16, 8 P.M.
Fri., May 17, 2 P.M.
Sat., May 18, 8 P.M.
Wolfgang Sawallisch, conductor
Maurizio Pollini, piano
MOZART Piano Concerto No. 27 in
    B-flat major, K. 595
SCHMIDT Symphony No. 2
Verizon Hall

Sat., May 18, 10 A.M., 11:15 A.M.,
    12:30 P.M.
Mon., May 20, 10 A.M., 11:15 A.M.
**Sound-All-Around
(for children ages 3–5)**
Academy of Music Ballroom

Thu., May 23, 8 P.M.
Fri., May 24, 2 P.M.
Sat., May 25, 8 P.M.
Tue., May 28, 8 P.M.
Wolfgang Sawallisch, conductor
MOZART "Gran Partita" Serenade (for
    13 wind instruments), K. 361
SCHOENBERG Transfigured Night
WAGNER Overture to *Tannhäuser*
Verizon Hall

Sun., May 26, 3 P.M.
Chamber Music Concert
Members of The Philadelphia
    Orchestra
STRAVINSKY Suite from
    A Soldier's Tale
HIGDON Zones (for percussion
    quartet and tape)
MOZART String Quintet No. 3, K. 516
Perelman Theater

Thu., May 30, 8 P.M.
Fri., May 31, 8 P.M.
Sat., June 1, 8 P.M.
Wolfgang Sawallisch, conductor
Jeffrey Khaner, flute
HAYDN Symphony No. 97
IBERT Flute Concerto
GRIEG Symphonic Dances, Op. 64
Verizon Hall

Thu., June 6, 8 P.M.
Fri., June 7, 2 P.M.
Sat., June 8, 8 P.M.
Mon., June 10, 8 P.M.
Wolfgang Sawallisch, conductor
Luba Orgonosova, soprano
Marjana Lipovšek, mezzo soprano
Stuart Neill, tenor
Carlo Colombara, bass
The Philadelphia Singers Chorale
    (David Hayes, music director)
VERDI Requiem
Verizon Hall

Sat., June 8, 11:30 A.M.
Family Concert:
"Music, Noise, and Silence"
Luis Biava, conductor
with Magic Circle Mime Company
Verizon Hall

Thu., June 13, 8 P.M.
Fri., June 14, 2 P.M.
Sat., June 15, 8 P.M.
Wolfgang Sawallisch, conductor
HIGDON Concerto for Orchestra
STRAUSS *Ein Heldenleben*
    (A Hero's Life)
Verizon Hall

For subscription information,
call 215-893-1955. For tickets
to individual performances,
call Ticket Philadelphia at
215-893-1999, visit the Box Office
at The Kimmel Center, or visit
www.philorch.org.

OPERA COMPANY OF PHILADELPHIA

Fri., Jan. 18, 8 P.M.
Sun., Jan. 20, 2:30 P.M.
Wed., Jan. 23, 7:30 P.M.
Fri., Jan. 25, 8 P.M.
Sun., Jan. 27, 2:30 P.M.
Wed., Jan. 30, 7:30 P.M.
Sat., Feb. 2, 2:30 P.M.
La Périchole
by Jacques Offenbach
Academy of Music

Fri., Mar. 1, 8 P.M.
Sun., Mar. 3, 2:30 P.M.
Wed., Mar. 6, 7:30 P.M.
Fri., Mar. 8, 8 P.M.
Sun., Mar. 10, 2:30 P.M.
Thu., Mar. 14, 7:30 P.M.
Sat., Mar. 16, 2:30 P.M.
Madama Butterfly
by Giacomo Puccini
Academy of Music

Fri., Mar. 15, 8 P.M.
Sun., Mar. 17, 2:30 P.M.
Wed., Mar. 20, 7:30 P.M.
Fri., Mar. 22, 8 P.M.
Sun., Mar. 24, 2:30 P.M.
Tue., Mar. 26, 7:30 P.M.
Sat., Mar. 30, 2:30 P.M.
Don Giovanni
by Wolfgang Amadeus Mozart
Academy of Music

Sun., April 7, 2:30 P.M.
Tue., April 9, 7:30 P.M.
Thu., April 11, 7:30 P.M.
Sat., April 13, 2:30 P.M.
Wed., April 17, 7:30 P.M.
Fri., April 19, 8 P.M.
Sun., April 21, 2:30 P.M.
The Capulets and the Montagues
by Vincenzo Bellini
Academy of Music

For subscription information,
call 215-732-8400. For tickets to
individual performances, call
Ticket Philadelphia at 215-893-1999
or visit the Box Office at the
Academy of Music.

PENNSYLVANIA BALLET

Fri., Feb. 8, 8 P.M.
Sat., Feb. 9, 2 P.M., 8 P.M.
Sun., Feb. 10, 2 P.M.
Thu., Feb. 14, 8 P.M.
Fri., Feb. 15, 8 P.M.
Sat., Feb. 16, 2 P.M., 8 P.M.
Sun., Feb. 17, 2 P.M.
Coppélia
Academy of Music

Wed., Mar. 13, 8 P.M.
Thu., Mar. 14, 8 P.M.
Fri., Mar. 15, 8 P.M.
Sat., Mar. 16, 8 P.M.
Sun., Mar. 17, 2 P.M.
Jerome Robbins, Interplay
Merriam Theater at the University of
the Arts

Fri., May 3, 8 P.M.
Sat., May 4, 2 P.M., 8 P.M.
Sun., May 5, 2 P.M.
Thu., May 9, 8 P.M.
Fri., May 10, 8 P.M.
Sat., May 11, 2 P.M., 8 P.M.
Sun., May 12, 2 P.M.
The Sleeping Beauty
Academy of Music

Wed., June 12, 8 P.M.
Thu., June 13, 8 P.M.
Fri., June 14, 8 P.M.
Sat., June 15, 2 P.M., 8 P.M.
Sun., June 16, 2 P.M.
Rodin, Mis en Vie
Merriam Theater at the
University of the Arts

For subscription information, call
215-551-7000. Tickets for individual
performances at the Merriam Theater
can be purchased by calling
TicketMaster at 215-336-2000.
Tickets for individual performances
at the Academy of Music can be
purchased by calling Ticket
Philadelphia at 215-893-1999,
visiting the Box Office at The
Kimmel Center, or online at
operaphilly.com.

AMERICAN THEATER ARTS FOR YOUTH

Tue., Feb. 19, 10 A.M., 12:15 P.M.
Wed., Feb. 20, 10 A.M., 12:15 P.M.
Thu., Feb. 21, 10 A.M., 12:15 P.M.
The Little Mermaid
Perelman Theater

Mon., Feb. 26, 10 A.M., 12:15 P.M.
Wizard of Oz
Perelman Theater

Sat., Mar. 2, 10:30 A.M., 12:30 P.M.
Mon., Mar. 4, 10 A.M., 12:15 P.M.
Tue., Mar. 5, 10 A.M., 12:15 P.M.
Wed., Mar. 6, 10 A.M., 12:15 P.M.
Beauty and the Beast
Perelman Theater

Wed., April 17, 10 A.M., 12:15 P.M.
Thu., April 18, 10 A.M., 12:15 P.M.
Fri., April 19, 10 A.M., 12:15 P.M.
Sat., April 20, 10:30 A.M., 12:30 P.M.
Alice in Wonderland
Perelman Theater

Mon., May 6, 10 A.M., 12:15 P.M.
Tue., May 7, 10 A.M., 12:15 P.M.
Sat., May 11, 10:30 A.M., 12:30 P.M.
Cinderella
Perelman Theater

Wed., May 8, 10 A.M., 12:15 P.M.
Fri., May 10, 10 A.M., 12:15 P.M.
Wizard of Oz
Perelman Theater

Thu., May 23, 10 A.M., 12:15 P.M.
Fri., May 24, 10 A.M., 12:15 P.M.
Tom Sawyer
Perelman Theater

*For more information, call
215-563-3501. For tickets, call
Ticket Philadelphia at
215-893-1999 or visit the
Box Office at The Kimmel Center.*

THE CHAMBER ORCHESTRA OF PHILADELPHIA

Sun., Jan. 6, 2:30 P.M.
Mon., Jan. 7, 7:30 P.M.
Ignat Solzhenitsyn, conductor
Sylvia McNair, soprano
Jon Humphrey, tenor
David Wilson-Johnson, bass
The Philadelphia Singers
    David Hayes, music director
HAYDN *The Creation*
    (Multimedia Production)
Perelman Theater

Sun., Feb. 10, 2:30 P.M.
Mon., Feb. 11, 7:30 P.M.
Ignat Solzhenitsyn, conductor
Steven Isserlis, cello
HINDEMITH Five Pieces
    for String Orchestra
TCHAIKOVSKY Variations on a
    Rococo Theme & Andante
    Cantabile
BEETHOVEN Symphony No. 7
    in A Major
Perelman Theater

Sun., Feb. 24, 2:30 P.M.
Mon., Feb. 25, 7:30 P.M.
Jeri Lynne Johnson, conductor
Jason Vieaux, guitar
Classical Music from the Movies
Perelman Theater

Sun., Mar. 24, 2:30 P.M.
Mon., Mar. 25, 7:30 P.M.
I Musici
VIVALDI *The Four Seasons*
    (Multimedia Production)
Perelman Theater

Sun., April 7, 2:30 P.M.
Mon., April 8, 7:30 P.M.
The Romeros Guitar Quartet
Maximiano Valdés, conductor
ZIPOLI Suite in B Minor
REVUELTAS Colvines for
    Chamber Orchestra
RODRIGO Concerto Andaluz
    for Four Guitars
MONCAYO Homage to Cervantes
VILLA-LOBOS Sinfoníetta No. 1
Perelman Theater

Sun., April 28, 2:30 P.M.
Mon., April 29, 7:30 P.M.
Otto-Werner Mueller, conductor
Susan Starr, piano
MOZART Symphony No. 35
    in D Major (Haffner)
MENDELSSOHN Piano Concerto
    No. 1 in G Minor
BEETHOVEN Symphony No. 8
    in F Major
Perelman Theater

Sun., May 19, 2:30 P.M.
Mon., May 20, 7:30 P.M.
Ignat Solzhenitsyn, conductor
Cho-Liang Lin, violin
BACH Orchestral Suite No. 2
    in B Minor
MOZART Violin Concerto No. 4
    in D Major
BRITTEN Simple Symphony
BACH Orchestral Suite No. 4
    in D Major
Perelman Theater

Sun., June 2, 2:30 P.M.
Mon., June 3, 7:30 P.M.
Ignat Solzhenitsyn, conductor
Gary Graffman, piano
BACH, Brandenburg Concerto No. 1
    in F Major
PRADO, Piano Concerto for the
    Left Hand (World Premiere)
MOZART, Symphony No. 38 in
    D Major (Prague)
Perelman Theater

*For subscription information,
call 215-545-5451 or visit
www.chamberorchestra.org. For tickets
to individual performances, call Ticket
Philadelphia at 215-893-1999 or visit
the Box Office at The Kimmel Center.*

THE PHILADELPHIA CHAMBER MUSIC SOCIETY

Tue., Jan. 15, 8 P.M.
Vermeer Quartet
Perelman Theater

Fri., Jan. 18, 8 P.M.
Miami String Quartet
Jaime Laredo, violin
Sharon Robinson, cello
Pennsylvania Convention Center
Auditorium

Sun., Jan. 20, 3 P.M.
Radu Lupu, piano
Perelman Theater

Fri., Jan. 25, 8 P.M.
Wolfgang Holzmair, baritone
Pennsylvania Convention Center
Auditorium

Fri., Feb. 1, 8 P.M.
Tokyo String Quartet
Perelman Theater

Wed., Feb. 6, 8 P.M.
Pamela Frank, violin
Claude Frank, piano
Perelman Theater

Fri., Feb. 15, 8 P.M.
Guarneri String Quartet
Perelman Theater

Fri., Feb. 22, 8 P.M.
Marietta Simpson, mezzo-soprano
*Cosponsored by the Musical Fund Society
of Philadelphia*
Perelman Theater

Tue., Feb. 19, 8 P.M.
Musicians from Marlboro
Perelman Theater

Sun., Feb. 24, 3 P.M.
Muir String Quartet
Pennsylvania Convention Center
Auditorium

Wed., Feb. 27, 8 P.M.
Juilliard String Quartet
Perelman Theater

Thu., Feb. 28, 8 P.M.
András Schiff, piano
Perelman Theater

Fri., Mar. 1, 8 P.M.
Regina Carter Quintet
Pennsylvania Convention Center
Auditorium

Tue., Mar. 5, 8 P.M.
Nathan Gunn, baritone
Perelman Theater

Wed., Mar. 6, 8 P.M.
PCMS Players I
Guarneri String Quartet
Claude Frank, Piano
Pennsylvania Convention Center
Auditorium

Thu., Mar. 7, 8 P.M.
Artemis Quartet
Pennsylvania Convention Center
Auditorium

Tue., Mar. 12, 8 P.M.
Musicians from Marlboro
Perelman Theater

Wed., Mar. 13, 8 P.M.
Midori, violin
Perelman Theater

Wed., Mar. 20, 8 P.M.
Beaux Arts Trio
Perelman Theater

Fri., Mar. 22, 8 P.M.
Brentano String Quartet
Samuel Rhodes, viola
Joel Krosnick, cello
Perelman Theater

Sat., Mar. 23, 8 P.M.
Arditti String Quartet
*Co-sponsored by the Musical Fund Society
of Philadelphia*
The Curtis Institute

Tue., April 2, 8 P.M.
American String Quartet
Lydia Artymiw, piano
David Soyer, cello
Pennsylvania Convention Center
Auditorium

Wed., April 3, 8 P.M.
Orion String Quartet
Ida Kavafian, viola
Perelman Theater

Fri., April 5, 8 P.M.
Richard Goode, piano
Perelman Theater

Wed., April 17, 8 P.M.
Elizabeth Futral, soprano
Perelman Theater

Fri., April 19, 8 P.M.
PCMS Players II
Johannes Quartet
Perelman Theater

Mon., April 22, 8 P.M.
PCMS Players III
Ignat Solzhenitsyn, Piano
Ida Levin, Violin
Peter Stumpf, Cello
Perelman Theater

Sun., May 3, 3 P.M.
Philadelphia Singers
*Cosponsored by the Musical Fund Society
of Philadelphia*
Pennsylvania Convention Center
Auditorium

Fri., May 10, 8 P.M.
Marc-André Hamelin, piano
Perelman Theater

Sun., May 12, 3 P.M.
Juilliard String Quartet
Pennsylvania Convention Center
Auditorium

*For subscriptions and information,
call 215-569-8080 or visit
www.pcmsnet.org. For tickets to
individual performances at Perelman
Theater, call Ticket Philadelphia at
215-893-1999 or visit the Box Office
at The Kimmel Center.*

PETER NERO AND THE PHILLY POPS®

Fri., Jan. 25, 8 P.M.
Sat., Jan. 26, 2 P.M.
Sun., Jan. 27, 3 P.M.
**A Richard Rodgers Songbook
with Maureen McGovern**
Verizon Hall

Fri., Feb. 22, 8 P.M.
Sat., Feb. 23, 2 P.M.
Sun., Feb. 24, 3 P.M.
**Broadway Showstoppers II
with Christiane Noll, Billy Porter,
and Keith Buterbaugh**
Verizon Hall

Sat., Mar. 30, 2 P.M., 8 P.M.
Sun., Mar. 31, 3 P.M.
**Sing Sing Swing!
with Ann Hampton Callaway**
Verizon Hall

Fri., May 3, 8 P.M.
Sat., May 4, 2 P.M.
Sun., May 5, 3 P.M.
**Celebrate America
with The Voices of The POPS**
Verizon Hall

*For subscription information,
call 215-546-6400. For tickets
to individual performances, call
Ticket Philadelphia at 215-893-1999
or visit the Box Office at The
Kimmel Center.*

GALA PREVIEW COMMITTEES

of The Kimmel Center for the Performing Arts

Preview Corporate Committee

William J. Avery, Co-Chair
Charles P. Connolly, Jr., Co-Chair

Stephen A. Cozen
Dave Davis
G. Fred DiBona, Jr.
John G. Drosdick
James B. Ginty
Rosemarie B. Greco
Richard J. Green
Robert Hall
Harold A. Honickman
Samuel P. Katz
Catherine M. Keating
Kenneth G. Lawrence
Herbert Lotman
Charles P. Pizzi
Alan L. Reid
Brian L. Roberts
George M. Ross
Ronald Rubin
Lawrence A. Weinbach
Daniel J. Whelan

Preview Production Committee

David G. Marshall, Chair

Kenneth Gamble
Lynne Honickman
Larry Magid
Sharon Pinkenson

Preview Marketing Committee

Lynne Honickman, Co-Chair
Brian P. Tierney, Co-Chair

Donna Boscia
Pamela Browner Crawley
Laurada Byers
Richard A. Doran
Fatimah Gamble
Trudy Haynes
Steven Korman
Fred Shabel
Molly D. Shepard
Norman Tissian

The Kimmel Center for the Performing Arts • December 14–15, 2001

LIST COMPLETE AS OF NOVEMBER 1, 2001

LEADERSHIP BENEFACTORS

THE SIDNEY KIMMEL FOUNDATION

PREMIUM BENEFACTORS

COMMERCE BANK

DELAWARE RIVER PORT AUTHORITY

DRINKER BIDDLE AND REATH

L.F. DRISCOLL CO.

FIRST UNION/WACHOVIA

MR. AND MRS. DAVID B. FORD

THE JAMES AND AGNES KIM FOUNDATION

LIBERTY PROPERTY TRUST

MERCK AND COMPANY

RUTH AND RAYMOND G. PERELMAN

PHILADELPHIA INQUIRER AND DAILY NEWS

UNISYS CORPORATION

BENEFACTORS

AMERICAN BUSINESS FINANCIAL SERVICES, INC.

AON

ARCHITECTURAL WOODWORKING/IMPERIAL WOODWORKING COMPANY

AT&T

ATOFINA CHEMICALS, INC.

WILLIAM J. AVERY

BALLARD, SPAHR, ANDREWS AND INGERSOLL, LLP

BANK OF AMERICA PRIVATE BANK

MR. AND MRS. DAVID J. BERKMAN

BERWIND CORPORATION

BLANK, ROME, COMISKY AND MCCAULEY

MR. AND MRS. J. MAHLON BUCK, JR.

BYERS' CHOICE LTD.

CIGNA CORPORATION

MR. AND MRS. TRISTRAM C. COLKET, JR.

THE COMCAST FAMILY OF COMPANIES

COZEN O'CONNOR

CROWN CORK AND SEAL COMPANY, INC.

FLEET BANK

PENNY AND BOB FOX

VERONICA GOLDBERG

CAROLE AND EMILIO GRAVAGNO

MRS. SAMUEL M.V. HAMILTON

LYNNE AND HAROLD HONICKMAN

J. P. MORGAN PRIVATE BANK

JONES APPAREL GROUP, INC.

THE KAISERMAN COMPANY

BERNICE R. KORMAN AND STEVEN H. KORMAN

KPMG CONSULTING

LINCOLN FINANCIAL GROUP

HERBERT AND KAREN LOTMAN

MANUGISTICS

TERRY ANN MAREK AND PETER BUTTENWEISER

DAVID G. AND SANDRA G. MARSHALL

MELLON FINANCIAL CORPORATION

MR. AND MRS. ALAN B. MILLER

LESLIE ANNE MILLER AND RICHARD B. WORLEY

MRS. J. MAXWELL MORAN

PECO ENERGY

PNC FINANCIAL SERVICES GROUP

PUBLIC FINANCIAL MANAGEMENT

RESOURCE AMERICA, INC.

LYN AND GEORGE ROSS

MR. AND MRS. WILLARD G. ROUSE III

RONALD AND MARCIA RUBIN

SAP AMERICA, INC.

CAROLE AND JOSEPH SHANIS

MOLLY D. SHEPARD AND GILLES E. RICHARD

STRAWBRIDGE'S

SUNOCO

UNIVERSITY OF PENNSYLVANIA

VERIZON

WOLF, BLOCK, SCHORR AND SOLIS-COHEN, LLP

WPVI-TV/6ABC

MR. AND MRS. ANDREW N. YAO

INDIVIDUAL BENEFACTORS

ACE INA HOLDINGS, INC.

DEAN ADLER AND SUSANNA LACHS ADLER

NINA AND BILLY ALBERT

GISELA AND DENNIS ALTER

THE ANNENBERG FOUNDATION

DR. AND MRS. HERBERT AXELROD

MR. AND MRS. RICHARD K. BARNHART

ANN R. BARUCH

FAHNYA AND DONALD BEAN

ELAINE AND VINCENT G. BELL, JR.

PETER A. BENOLIEL

THE BINSWANGER FOUNDATION

MR. AND MRS. ALAN D. BLEZNAK

WAYNE AND SHEREE BLOCH

CHARLES W. BOWDEN, JR., AND DR. ELIZABETH BOWDEN

JENNE K. BRITELL, PH.D.

JULIE AND ROBERT BRYAN

MR. AND MRS. ALEXANDER K. BUCK

MR. AND MRS. WILLIAM C. BUCK

BUNUE ELUILI FOUNDATION

LAURADA BYERS

THE DONALD R. CALDWELL FAMILY

JANE F. CARTON

MR. AND MRS. JOSEPH L. CASTLE II

LUCILLE AND ANDREW CAVITOLO

SCOTT AND NELLY CHILDRESS

CATHERINE R. AND ANTHONY A. CLIFTON

MR. AND MRS. CHARLES P. CONNOLLY, JR.

MR. AND MRS. M. TODD COOKE

HILARY AND RICHARD COOPER

SUSAN AND JEREMY COOTE

SARAH AND FRANK COULSON

DANELLA CONSTRUCTION CORPORATION

MR. AND MRS. RODNEY D. DAY III

MR. AND MRS. FRANCIS WILLIAM DE SERIO

RICHARD DILSHEIMER AND BARBARA EBERLEIN

DOBSON PIPE ORGAN BUILDERS, LTD.

TANIA AND CRAIG DRAKE

GOVERNOR AND MRS. PIERRE S. DU PONT IV

MR. AND MRS. THOMAS P. EMMONS

C. ERICKSON AND SONS

ERNST AND YOUNG LLP

CATHERINE AND PETER ERNSTER

MR. AND MRS. WALTER FARNAM

JOSEPH AND MARY FENKEL

JAIMIE AND DAVID FIELD

JOSEPH AND MARIE FIELD

MARTIN AND KATHLEEN FIELD

MR. AND MRS. EUGENE C. FISH

MR. AND MRS. RICHARD J. FOX

MR. AND MRS. JACK M. FRIEDLAND

EUGENE AND CATHERYNE GARFIELD, EUGENE GARFIELD FOUNDATION

TONI AND BOB GARRISON

JAMES GARRAWAY, II

NANCY AND BILL GILES

MR. AND MRS. MILTON GINSBURG

HOWARD GITTIS

DR. ALFRED E. AND ADELE GOLDMAN

CECILIA AND OLIVER D. GOLDMAN

MS. JULIET J. GOODFRIEND AND DR. MARC R. MOREAU

THOMAS AND SUZANNE GORMAN

GREATER PHILADELPHIA CHAMBER OF COMMERCE

MARLA AND RICHARD GREEN

MR. AND MRS. GERALD GUSHNER

MARY BERT AND ALVIN P. GUTMAN

JOHN C. AND CHARA C. HAAS

MRS. GWATHMEY HARRIS

MR. AND MRS. ROBERT HAUPTFUHRER

HAYDEN REAL ESTATE

HENKEL FAMILY

SUSAN O. W. AND HON. PAUL L. JAFFE

JERRY L. AND RAYE E. JOHNSON

JOAN AND VICTOR L. JOHNSON

HENRY K. AND HELEN M. JUSTI

LISA D. KABNICK

MATTHEW H. AND ELIZABETH G. KAMENS

ANDREA AND WARREN KANTOR

CONNIE AND SAM KATZ, GREATER PHILADELPHIA FIRST

DR. HERBERT KEAN AND HON. JOYCE S. KEAN

MR. AND MRS. LAWRENCE J. KENT

MR. AND MRS. LEONARD KLEHR

MIRIAM KLEIN

STEPHEN KLEIN AND DIANE GIUNTA

JOSEPH H. KLUGER AND SUSAN LEWIS

DRS. CAROLINE AND PETER KOLLMEYER

BERNICE J. AND JOSEPH K. KOPLIN

JANE AND LEONARD KORMAN

H. F. (GERRY) AND MARGUERITE LENFEST

ELAINE LEVITT AND JOEL GERSHMAN

IRA LUBERT

MR. AND MRS. CRAWFORD C. MADEIRA, JR.

MR. AND MRS. A. BRUCE MAINWARING

MIRIAM AND SONNY MANDELL

THE MARCUS FAMILY FOUNDATION

FAMILY MAYER FOUNDATION

MR. AND MRS. SAMUEL A. MCCULLOUGH

MRS. GEORGE MCFARLAND

MARTHA MCGEARY SNIDER

CRAIG AND MICHELE MILLARD

LADDIE AND LINDA MONTAGUE

ROBERT E. MORTENSEN

JEANETTE LERMAN NEUBAUER AND JOSEPH NEUBAUER

NEWMAN AND COMPANY, INC.

NORFOLK SOUTHERN CORPORATION

ARTIS T. ORE

JEFFREY P. ORLEANS CHARITABLE FOUNDATION

DAWN AND DON PAPARONE

MR. AND MRS. THOMAS N. PAPPAS

PARKWAY CORPORATION

STUART AND VIRGINIA PELTZ

JANE G. PEPPER

THE PHILADELPHIA EAGLES

PIRELLI HIGH VOLTAGE CABLES AND SYSTEMS

THE DAVID H. PLEET FOUNDATION

MARGO AND DANIEL POLETT

LORRAINE AND DAVID POPOWICH

JUDY POTE

PRICEWATERHOUSECOOPERS

LOUISE H. AND ALAN L. REED

MR. AND MRS. MARC J. RICHMAN

GABRIELLE AND AL RINALDI, JACOBS MUSIC

DR. AND MRS. AURELIANO RIVAS

LISA G. ROBERTS AND DAVID SELTZER

MILTON L. ROCK AND CONSTANCE W. BENOLIEL

WENDY AND PAUL ROSEN

DAVID B. RUBENSTEIN AND MICHELE A. KREISLER

MARK E. RUBENSTEIN

SAKS FIFTH AVENUE

THE ETHEL AND JACK SANDMAN CHARITABLE TRUST

ADELE AND HAROLD SCHAEFFER

GARY AND RUTHANNE SCHLARBAUM

ANDREW SCHLESSINGER

MR. AND MRS. THEODORE H. SEIDENBERG

LYNN AND HOWARD SHECTER

RICHARD AND BETSY SHEERR

MR. AND MRS. JOHN J. F. SHERRERD

MOLLIE AND FRANK SLATTERY

WILLIAM A. SLAUGHTER

MR. AND MRS. RICHARD L. SMOOT

CONSTANCE AND JOSEPH SMUKLER

EDWARD SNIDER

MYUNG AND YOUNG SIM SONG

HAROLD AND ANN SORGENTI

JOAN AND BERNARD SPAIN

MR. AND MRS. HARMON S. SPOLAN

MR. AND MRS. ROBERT L. STEVENS

ILIANA AND BEN STRAUSS

MR. AND MRS. JAMES B. STRAW

JANE C. AND THOMAS J. SULLIVAN III

SYLK CHARITABLE TRUST

MR. AND MRS. SCOTT TARTE

MR. AND MRS. BRUCE E. TOLL

TRUE NORTH FOUNDATION

UTILITY LINE SERVICE

WILLIAM AND LORINE VOGT

JUDEE VON SELDENECK

STEPHEN TODD WALKER AND DOROTHY SCHADE WALKER

ALAN AND LAURA WECHSLER

JOSEPH WEISS AND SHARON PINKENSON

LARRY AND HARRIET WEISS

MR. AND MRS. RAY WESTPHAL

SANKEY AND CONSTANCE WILLIAMS

WILMINGTON TRUST

BARBARA B. AND J. LAWRENCE WILSON

SONIA AND ROBERT WOLDOW

MARGERY S. WOLF

RICHARD E. WOOSNAM AND DIANE DALTO

IN MEMORY OF DR. AND MRS. J. BENJAMIN YASINOW

ZELDIN AND GUEST

JAMES W. AND DEBORA C. ZUG

ONE ANONYMOUS

THE CAMPAIGN TO BUILD THE KIMMEL CENTER

LIST COMPLETE AS OF NOVEMBER 1, 2001

PRINCIPAL FOUNDERS

$30,000,000+

THE SIDNEY KIMMEL FOUNDATION
COMMONWEALTH OF PENNSYLVANIA
CITY OF PHILADELPHIA

$5,000,000+

MRS. SAMUEL M. V. HAMILTON
THE WILLIAM PENN FOUNDATION
RUTH AND RAYMOND G. PERELMAN
VERIZON
ONE ANONYMOUS

$2,000,000+

CIGNA CORPORATION
COMCAST CORPORATION/COMCAST CABLE/COMCAST-SPECTACOR/QVC
DELAWARE RIVER PORT AUTHORITY
FIRST UNION/WACHOVIA
F. OTTO HAAS CHARITABLE TRUST
INDEPENDENCE FOUNDATION
THE KRESGE FOUNDATION
MERCK & COMPANY, INC.
SUNOCO

$250,000+

ACE INA Holdings, Inc.

AT&T Foundation

ATOFINA Chemicals, Inc.

Mr. and Mrs. Vincent G.
Bell, Jr.

Alan and Kathleen Bleznak

The Boeing Company

Mr. and Mrs. Charles W.
Bowden, Jr.

Bristol-Myers Squibb Company

Mr. and Mrs. Julian Brodsky

Mr. and Mrs. Alexander K. Buck

Mr. and Mrs. William C. Buck

The Donald R. Caldwell Family

Mr. and Mrs. Joseph L. Castle

CertainTeed Corportation,
A Saint-Gobain Company

Scott and Nelly Childress

CMS Companies

Mr. and Mrs. Tristram C.
Colket, Jr.

The Connelly Foundation

Conrail Inc.

Corestates

Sarah and Frank Coulson

Cozen O'Connor

Evelyn S. and Rodney D. Day, III

Mr. and Mrs. Francis W.
De Serio

Farber Foundation

Eugene Feiner Foundation

The Joseph and Marie Field
Foundation

General Accident Insurance

The Greenewalt Estate

The Grundy Foundation

The Hassel Foundation

Lynne and Harold Honickman

Charles Lukens Huston
Foundation

Lynn Benoliel Jacobson

Karr-Barth Associates/AXA
Foundation

Dr. Herbert Kean and
Hon. Joyce S. Kean

Norma and Leonard Klorfine
Foundation

Hyman Korman Family
Foundation

Elaine Levitt and Joel Gershman

Samuel P. Mandell Foundation

Sandra G. and David G.
Marshall

Meridian Bancorp, Inc.

Jill and Alan B. Miller

Morgan Stanley Asset
Management Company

Mr. and Mrs. Pete and
Hillary Musser

Ron and Suzanne Naples

Mr. and Mrs. John B. Neff

Roy and Rosalind Neff

Mrs. Eugene Ormandy

Rite Aid Corporation

Ronald and Marcia Rubin

Safeguard Scientifics, Inc.

Carole and Joseph Shanis

Smukler-Lasch Family Trust

The Strauss Foundation

Strawbridge's

Toll Brothers, Inc.

US Airways

Larry and Harriet Weiss

WYETH

Mr. and Mrs. Andrew N. Yao

In memory of Herman and
Lee Zuritsky

One Anonymous

Century Club

$100,000+

Mr. and Mrs. Leonard
Abramson

Acme Markets, Inc.

AETNA U.S. Healthcare

Lorraine and Ben Alexander

The Armstrong Foundation

Arronson Foundation

William J. and Sharon L. Avery

Beneficia Foundation

David Berger

Berwind Corporation

Donna and Jon Boscia

Mr. and Mrs. Theodore A.
Burtis

Byers' Choice Ltd.

Mr. and Mrs. George M.
Cheston

Mr. and Mrs. John Gilray
Christy

Mr. and Mrs. M. Todd Cooke

Margaret Drake

Esther B. Dunlap

Gov. and Mrs. Pierre S.
du Pont IV

Catheryne and Eugene Garfield

Goldman, Sachs & Co.

Gray Charitable Trust

Mary Bert and Alvin P. Gutman

William A. Loeb

R. Gordon McGovern

The McLean Contributionship

Mr. and Mrs. H. Laddie
Montague, Jr.

Elizabeth R. Moran

Oki Data Americas, Inc.

Orleans Homebuilders

The Ounsworth Family

Pennoni Associates Inc.

Philadelphia Gas Works

Philadelphia Inquirer and
Daily News

Philadelphia Marriott and Host
Marriott Corporation

Mr. and Mrs. Frank N. Piasecki

The David H. Pleet Foundation

Provident Mutual Life
Insurance Company

Quaker Chemical Corporation

Reliance Insurance Group

Al and Gabrielle Rinaldi, Jacobs
Music Company

Milton L. Rock and Constance
W. Benoliel

Mr. and Mrs. Joseph W.
Rogers, Jr.

Maestro Wolfgang Sawallisch

Mr. and Mrs. John J. F. Sherrerd

Teleflex Incorporated

Dr. and Dr. John M.
Templeton, Jr.

Mr. and Mrs. Brian P. Tierney

The Tuttleman Family
Foundation, Edna and
Stan Tuttleman

Mrs. Samuel B. Vrooman III

Wawa, Inc.

Wilmington Trust Company

Elizabeth G. Woodward

Legacy Club

$50,000+

Constance L. Abrams and
Ann G. Verber

Dean S. Adler and Susanna
Lachs Adler

Mrs. Gustave G. Amsterdam

Diane K. Apfelbaum

Ann R. Baruch

Mr. and Mrs. David J. Berkman

Cecilie and Eugene Block

Jill and Sheldon Bonovitz

Nora Mead Brownell

Grace K. Buck

Mr. and Mrs. James M. Buck III

Mr. and Mrs. Roland K.
Bullard, II

Margaret Lowry Butler

Louis N. Cassett Foundation

Mr. and Mrs. Jeremy Coote

Mr. and Mrs. Michael Dean

Richard Dilsheimer and
Barbara Eberlein

Mr. and Mrs. Craig M. Drake

Mr. and Mrs. John G. Drosdick

Duane, Morris and Heckscher

Ernst & Young LLP

Fleet Bank

MR. AND MRS. KENNETH GAMBLE

MRS. WILLIAM GERSTLEY II

JULIET J. GOODFRIEND AND
MARC R. MOREAU

MR. AND MRS. KENNETH N.
GOLDENBERG

THE GRAHAM COMPANY

ROSEMARIE B. GRECO

GRETE AND MARTYN GREENACRE

MR. AND MRS. ROBERT P.
HAUPTFUHRER

HOLT CARGO SYSTEMS

ARTHUR M. KAPLAN, ESQ., AND
R. DUANE PERRY

MR. AND MRS. ROBERT E.
KEITH, JR.

KLEHR, HARRISON, HARVEY,
BRANZBURG AND ELLERS

JOSEPH H. KLUGER AND
SUSAN E. LEWIS

ELENA AND FREDERICK KYLE

SONDRA AND MARTIN LANDES, JR.

THE LEEWAY FOUNDATION

S. GERALD AND ARLENE F. LITVIN

DR. AND MRS. FRANCIS MANLOVE

PEGGY AND JAMES E. MARKS
FOUNDATION

MARGARETT F. AND SAM S. MCKEEL

MILLER, ANDERSON AND SHERRERD

THE LEO MODEL FOUNDATION

ROBERT E. MORTENSEN

MOTHERS WORK, INC.

MAESTRO AND MRS. RICCARDO
MUTI

MUTI TRIBUTE BENEFIT CONCERT

STEPHANIE AND MICHAEL NAIDOFF

PAGLIACCI BENEFIT CONCERT

PENN DETROIT DIESEL-ALLISON

THE PHILADELPHIA ORCHESTRA
MUSICIANS

THE PHILADELPHIA ORCHESTRA
STAFF

LORRAINE AND DAVID POPOWICH

MR. AND MRS. SEYMOUR S.
PRESTON, III

FREDERIC AND ZORA PRYOR

LOUISE H. AND ALAN L. REED

MIDGE AND ED RENDELL

MR. AND MRS. PAUL ROSEN

MR. AND MRS. HAROLD S.
ROSENBLUTH

ZOE AND RICHARD RUEDA/TRANS
FREIGHT SYSTEMS, INC.

ROBERT MONTGOMERY SCOTT

RUTH RADBILL SCOTT

MR. AND MRS. PETER A. SEARS

MR. AND MRS. J. LAWRENCE SHANE

MOLLY D. SHEPARD AND
GILLES E. RICHARD

HAROLD A. AND ANN R. SORGENTI

MANUEL N. STAMATAKIS

LEON AND EMILY SUNSTEIN

TARGET STORES

THE WACHS, BOOK, AND
WEINGARTEN FAMILIES

BENNETT AND JUDITH WEINSTOCK

MR. JOSEPH H. WEISS AND
MS. SHARON PINKENSON

SANKEY AND CONSTANCE WILLIAMS

ESTATE OF MRS. GEORGE
WOODWARD

RICHARD E. WOOSNAM

LYNN AND PAUL YEAKEL

JAMES W. AND DEBORA C. ZUG

SPECIAL GIFTS
AND TAKE A SEAT

$15,000+

LINDA LEE ALTER AND SEYMOUR
MEDNICK

CATHERINE APOTHAKER

APS BENEFIT CONCERT

ARTHUR ANDERSEN LLP

KEVIN AUERBACH

ELLEN AND PHILLIP H. BAER

EILEEN BAIRD

HELEN GROOME BEATTY TRUST

THE BINSWANGER FOUNDATION

MR. AND MRS. JAMES F. BODINE

SALLY AND DICK BRICKMAN

MR. AND MRS. IRA BRIND

BARBARA CANTOR

CHURCHILL FAMILY FOUNDATION

MR. AND MRS. SYLVAN M. COHEN

GIANNE P. CONARD

ANNE M. CONGDON

DAY & ZIMMERMANN, INC.

MR. AND MRS. MARK DICHTER

MR. AND MRS. F. EUGENE
DIXON, JR.

GLORIA DOEHLING AND JIM TAPLEY

DOLFINGER-MCMAHON
FOUNDATION

ABRAHAM M. AND ROSE ELLIS
FOUNDATION

MR. AND MRS. THOMAS P. EMMONS

PATRICK AND EVELYN GAGE

MR. AND MRS. WALTER B.
GALLAGHER

MR. AND MRS. CHARLES D.
GRAHAM, JR.

HARBOR CONSULTING AND
MANAGEMENT COMPANY

HEINEKEN USA, INC.

HERCULES INCORPORATED

JUDITH R. HYMAN

SUSAN O. W. AND
HON. PAUL L. JAFFE

HON. BRUCE W. KAUFFMAN

PAUL E. KELLY, JR.

JANE H. KESSON

JO ANN KLEIN

DR. AND MRS. MORTON M.
KLIGERMAN

DRS. ALBERT AND LORRAINE
KLIGMAN

LEO AND ED KNETZGER

JOSEPH K. AND BERNICE J. KOPLIN

TOBY DIANE KORMAN

LUANN C. KRESSLER

MRS. JOHN B. LEAKE

DR. AND MRS. WALTER P. LOMAX

MRS. CONSTANCE C. MOORE

MR. AND MRS. RAY B. MUNDT

MRS. MARLIN P. NELSON

DR. AND MRS. R. BARRETT NOONE

MR. AND MRS. JEREMIAH P.
O'GRADY

MR. AND MRS. SHAUN F. O'MALLEY

MR. AND MRS. HENRY E. ORYSIEK

MARY S. PAGE

PHILADELPHIA SUBURBAN WATER
COMPANY

MR. AND MRS. ROBERT POLLACK

DR. AND MRS. JOEL PORTER

MICHAEL AND SHERYL POULS

MR. AND MRS. ALFRED RAUCH, JR.

BOB AND LANNY REID

DR. AND MRS. AURELIANO RIVAS

MR. AND MRS. NORMAN P.
ROBINSON

MRS. F. ROBERT SAMUELS

THE ETHEL AND JACK SANDMAN
CHARITABLE TRUST

HELEN SCHWARTZ

BETSY AND RICHARD SHEERR

MR. AND MRS. SAMUEL SIDEWATER

SNIDER FOUNDATION

ESTATE OF MARIE M. OTTELLIUOS

MR. AND MRS. PETER S.
STRAWBRIDGE

MR. AND MRS. WILSON H. TAYLOR

MARTY TUZMAN

ESTATE OF EVELYN TYSON

MRS. FRANCIS L. VAN DUSEN

DANIEL AND MARILYN VEBER

JUDEE VON SELDENECK

BETTYRUTH WALTER, PH.D.

ESTHER C. AND PAUL H. WEIL
FOUNDATION

MR. AND MRS. RAINER WESTPHAL

GLEN AND TONYA WILSON

MR. AND MRS. ROBERT B. WOLF

WOLF, BLOCK, SCHORR &
SOLIS-COHEN LLP

MR. AND MRS. MARTIN J. ZELDIN

THREE ANONYMOUS

ARTISTS CIRCLE

$10,000+

AL AND JEANNE ABRAMS

MR. AND MRS. ROBERT S. APPLEBY

DR. EVA ARONFREED

MR. JOHN A. BAIRD, JR.

MR. AND MRS. ROBERT J. BUTERA

RHONDA AND DAVID COHEN

MR. AND MRS. DAVID P. EASTBURN

MR. AND MRS. ROBERT I. FINE

MR. AND MRS. JAMES B. GINTY

MR. AND MRS. DAVID GIRARD-DICARLO

HERMAN GOLDMAN FOUNDATION

ESTATE OF BERDA M. GOLDSMITH

DR. AND MRS. F. SHELDON HACKNEY

MR. AND MRS. H. EDWARD HANWAY

MARTIN A. HECKSCHER, ESQ.

WILLIAM M. HOLLENBACK, JR.

HOME DEPOT

MR. AND MRS. L. STOCKTON ILLOWAY

MR. ROBERT KLEIN AND MRS. JUDITH AURITT KLEIN

RICHARD AND TAIKO KRZYZANOWSKI

MR. AND MRS. EDWARD B. LEISENRING, JR.

THOMAS B. MACCABE, JR.

MR. AND MRS. ROBERT MCCLEMENTS, JR.

EDWARD A. MONTGOMERY, JR.

MR. AND MRS. ARTHUR C. MORTON

MR. AND MRS. DAVID PINCUS

MR. AND MRS. ISADORE SCOTT

IRENE AND FRED SHABEL

MARY L. SMITH

JAMES A. STERN

MR. AND MRS. GEORGE T. STEWART

SHELDON L. AND KAREN B. THOMPSON

MR. AND MRS. RICHARD J. WALSH

MR. AND MRS. A. MORRIS WILLIAMS, JR.

BENEFACTORS

$5,000+

MRS. JANE ABRAHAMS

ACADEMY OF MUSIC OF PHILADELPHIA, INC.

ARLIN AND NEYSA ADAMS

MS. LILLIAN AXE

MRS. ARDIS J. BLENKO

MR. AND MRS. DONALD B. BLENKO

JULIUS AND RAY CHARLESTEIN FOUNDATION

TED AND EMILY DAESCHLER

JUDITH FRANKFURT

MR. AND MRS. HAROLD FRIEDLAND

ELIZABETH P. GLENDINNING

MR. JOEL GREENBERG AND MS. MARCY GRINGLAS

ELIZABETH KAPNEK GRENALD

MR. AND MRS. JOHN B. HAGNER

HATFIELD MEMORIAL FUND

DR. AND MRS. PETER LAIBSON

MR. H. GATES LLOYD

MR. ANTHONY M. MARINO

MR. AND MRS. ROBERT C. MCADOO

DR. AND MRS. THOMAS M. MCMILLAN

MR. AND MRS. LOUIS MESHON

MR. AND MRS. EDWARD A. MONTGOMERY

MR. AND MRS. A. H. NISHIKAWA

MR. AND MRS. JAMES NOLEN

MRS. G. WILLING PEPPER

MR. AND MRS. WILLIAM R. PEPPER

MS. BEATRICE PITCAIRN

PQ CORPORATION

PRICEWATERHOUSECOOPERS

MR. AND MRS. NEIL C. RANDALL

MR. AND MRS. RICHARD S. RAVENSCROFT

MR. AND MRS. R. CARL RHOADS

THE RICHARDSON COMPANY

ROBERTS FOUNDATION

MR. RICHARD RUBENSTEIN

MR. AND MRS. PAUL R. RUBINCAM, JR.

SAUL, EWING, REMICK AND SAUL

MR. AND MRS. GEORGE H. SHAEFFER

DONALD U. SMITH AND H. HETHERINGTON SMITH

MR. MARK E. STALNECKER

LEE STEINBERG

MS. ROSEMARY C. SULLIVAN

MR. HENDERSON SUPPLEE III

MR. AND MRS. KENNETH S. SWEET, JR.

MR. HOWARD TURNER

MR. AND MRS. HUGH F. WALSH, JR.

AILEEN AND JULES WHITMAN

ONE ANONYMOUS

PARTNERS

$2,500+

MR. AND MRS. IRA ALBOM

MR. JOHN R. ALCHIN

BALIS & CO., INC.

WENDY BEETLESTONE

MR. AND MRS. ROBERT BLUM

MR. ROBERT W. BOGLE

DR. AND MRS. STANLEY L. BROWN

MR. JOHN J. BURNS

MR. AND MRS. J. PATRICK CARPENTER

CATHERS & ASSOCIATES, INC.

MS. BARBARA CHRYST

MS. CORDELIA CLEMENT

COMPTON FOUNDATION

MS. JEANNE M. DALTON

MARTIN J. DEWITT

DOBKIN FAMILY FOUNDATION

THE ELIZABETH M. DWYER MEMORIAL

MR. AND MRS. BERNARD EIZEN

DAVID AND PEGGY ELDER

MS. BARBARA EVANS

EDWARD T. FITZPATRICK, OSFS

MR. AND MRS. WILLIAM W. FOX, JR.

MR. AND MRS. ROBERT P. FRANKEL

MS. JUDITH FRANKFURT AND MR. JAMES OESTREICH

MR. AND MRS. PETER J. FREYD

SANDRA DUNGEE GLENN

DR. AND MRS. RICHARD B. GOULD

DR. AND MRS. MICHEL HOESSLY

MELANIE HOPKINS

MR. AND MRS. BOB HUTH

MR. BERNARD JACOBSON

MS. SUSAN E. KANE

ESTATE OF MARIA KORNGOLD

MR. AND MRS. MICHAEL E. MALONE

MR. RICHARD MENSCHEL

MR. AND MRS. JOHN A. NYHEIM

MR. JAMES P. O'BRIEN

MRS. FRANK J. O'MALLEY

MR. AND MRS. FRANCIS J. PIASTA

DR. AND MRS. JAY ROSAN

THE ROSS FAMILY FOUNDATION

ROTARY FOUNDATION OF PHILADELPHIA

MR. GARY SEGAL

MR. AND MRS. DANIEL F. SNEBERGER

MS. CORINNE STONE

DR. RICHARD SUMMERS AND MS. RONNIE BLOOM

SYLK CHARITABLE TRUST

JOE M. THOMSON

MS. LORRAINE TRUTEN

HOWARD VERLIN AND JINOUS KAZEMI-VERLIN

DR. HARLAN F. WEISMAN

GEORGE P. WHITE

PACESETTERS

$1,000+

DR. RAMESH RENUKA ADIRAJU

MR. DANIEL AHEARN, SR.

MR. AND MRS. GEORGE M. AHRENS

MR. KENNETH C. ALLEN

MR. AND MRS. HARRIS C. ALLER, JR.

MR. THOMAS ANGELL

The Kimmel Center for the Performing Arts

RAFAEL VIÑOLY ARCHITECTS, PC
RAFAEL VIÑOLY, PRINCIPAL
ARCHITECT

ARTEC CONSULTANTS, INC.
RUSSELL JOHNSON, PRESIDENT
ACOUSTICAL DESIGNER

THEATRE PROJECTS CONSULTANTS
RICHARD PILBROW, CHAIR
THEATER DESIGN CONSULTANTS

L.F. DRISCOLL CO./ARTIS T. ORE, INC.,
JOINT VENTURE PARTNERSHIP
JOHN DONNELLY, PRESIDENT
CONSTRUCTION MANAGER

ADELPHIA GRAPHIC SYSTEMS
SUBCONTRACTOR

AEI ELECTRIC COMPANY
SUBCONTRACTOR

AGGLETON & ASSOCIATES
SECURITY CONSULTANT

ALMOND GLASS WORKS
SUBCONTRACTOR

AMERICAN STAIR COMPANY
SUBCONTRACTOR

ANG ENGINEERING
CIVIL ENGINEER

ARCHITECTURAL SKYLIGHT
CO., INC.
SUBCONTRACTOR

ARCHITECTURAL
WOODWORKING INDUSTRIES
SUBCONTRACTOR

OVE ARUP & PARTNERS
MECHANICAL CONSULTANT

AVALOTIS
SUBCONTRACTOR

BAYSHORE REBAR, INC.
SUBCONTRACTOR

BELFI BROTHERS
SUBCONTRACTOR

JOHN F. BRENNAN, INC.
SUBCONTRACTOR

BUCHART-HORN, INC.
PA CONSULTANT

A. T. CHADWICK
SUBCONTRACTOR

CHILTON ENGINEERING
STRUCTURAL CONSULTANT

CINI-LITTLE INTERNATIONAL
FOOD SERVICE CONSULTANT

CITY OF PHILADELPHIA,
DEPARTMENT OF AFFIRMATIVE
ACTION
CHARLES E. THORPE, MBE
COORDINATOR
*AFFIRMATIVE ACTION
OVERSIGHT COMMITTEE*

CITY OF PHILADELPHIA,
DEPARTMENT OF LICENSES &
INSPECTIONS
HING WAN LUI, P.E., BUILDING
PLAN EXAMINER
L & I PLAN EXAMINER

J. R. CLANCY, INC.
SUBCONTRACTOR

COMMONWEALTH OF
PENNSYLVANIA,
OFFICE OF THE BUDGET
RICHARD DREHER, PROGRAM
MANAGER
CONTROLLER

CONSPEC SYSTEMS, INC.
SUBCONTRACTOR

D'ANGELO BROTHERS
SUBCONTRACTOR

DEWHURST MACFARLANE &
PARTNERS
STRUCTURAL CONSULTANT

DOBSON PIPE ORGAN
BUILDERS
ORGAN CONSULTANT

EDA ROOFING CORPORATION
SUBCONTRACTOR

CLAUDE ENGLE LIGHTING
DESIGN
CONSULTANT

EWING COLE
INTERIOR DESIGNER

FLYNN FLOORS, INC.
SUBCONTRACTOR

GALA THEATER EQUIPMENT
SUBCONTRACTOR

HERMAN GOLDNER COMPANY
SUBCONTRACTOR

GOLDREICH ENGINEERING
STRUCTURAL CONSULTANT

GORDON GROUP
SUBCONTRACTOR

GREATER PHILADELPHIA URBAN
AFFAIRS COALITION
*AFFIRMATIVE ACTION
OVERSIGHT COMMITTEE*

HAVERTY MILLWORK
CORPORATION
SUBCONTRACTOR

HELMARK STEEL, INC.
SUBCONTRACTOR

HOFFEND & SONS, INC.
SUBCONTRACTOR

HUGHES & ASSOCIATES
LIFE SAFETY CONSULTANT

INDEPENDENT BALANCING
COMPANY
SUBCONTRACTOR

IRWIN SEATING COMPANY
SUBCONTRACTOR

JGL MANAGEMENT SERVICES
COMPANY
FOOD SERVICE CONSULTANT

LEPORE/MARK CONTRACTORS,
JOINT VENTURE
SUBCONTRACTOR

MARSH USA, INC.
OCIP CONSULTANT

MARYLAND SOUND & IMAGE
SUBCONTRACTOR

MCCLYMONT & RAK
GEOTECHNICAL CONSULTANT

MOMETALS, INC.
SUBCONTRACTOR

MONARCH INDUSTRIES, INC.
SUBCONTRACTOR

NATIONAL GLASS & METAL CO.
SUBCONTRACTOR

NORTHSTAR FIRE PROTECTION
SUBCONTRACTOR

O'BRIEN BUSINESS SYSTEMS,
INC.
SUBCONTRACTOR

DESIGN INTERIOR PLANTSCAPE
SUBCONTRACTOR

PERKS-REUTTER ASSOCIATES
CONSULTANT

PHILADELPHIA DUGGAN &
MARCON
SUBCONTRACTOR

PHILADELPHIA INDUSTRIAL
DEVELOPMENT CORPORATION
PHILADELPHIA CONSULTANT

PIETRINI & SONS
SUBCONTRACTOR

PWI ENGINEERING
MECHANICAL CONSULTANT

RIDGWAY'S
BLUEPRINT REPRODUCTION

SCHAFFER, DESOUZA, BROWN
SUBCONTRACTOR

SCHNADER, HARRISON, SEGAL
& LEWIS
PROJECT LAW FIRM

ROBERT SCHWARTZ &
ASSOCIATES
SPECIFICATION CONSULTANT

SSM INDUSTRIES
SUBCONTRACTOR

THORNE EQUIPMENT COMPANY
SUBCONTRACTOR

THORNTON TOMASETTI
ENGINEERS
STRUCTURAL CONSULTANT

THYSSEN ELEVATOR
SUBCONTRACTOR

TRACORP
SUBCONTRACTOR

TRAVELERS INSURANCE
INSURANCE CARRIER

U.S. PROFESSIONAL
LABORATORIES, INC.
INSPECTION AGENCY

VAN DEUSEN & ASSOCIATES
*VERTICAL TRANSPORTATION
CONSULTANT*

WATER CONTROL ENGINEERING
SUBCONTRACTOR

WILLIARD, INC.
SUBCONTRACTOR

WILSON, IHRIG & ASSOCIATES,
INC.
THEATER CONSULTANT

WOJCIECHOWSKI DESIGN
GRAPHIC DESIGN CONSULTANT

Staff

LESLIE ANNE MILLER, PRESIDENT

ADMINISTRATION

NANCY WALKER ROGERS, DIRECTOR OF ADMINISTRATION

CONSTANCE ABRAMS, CONSULTANT

CAROLANN IVERS, DIRECTOR OF HUMAN RESOURCES

ELLEN HUTTON, EXECUTIVE ASSISTANT

LISA NARDO, ADMINISTRATIVE ASSISTANT

JENNIFER GORDON, RECEPTIONIST

CONSTRUCTION

GEORGE SHAEFFER, PROJECT MANAGER

DEVELOPMENT

JUDITH R. HYMAN, DIRECTOR OF DEVELOPMENT

MELISSA COOPERSMITH, DIRECTOR OF MAJOR GIFTS

NANCY PLUM, DIRECTOR OF FOUNDATION RELATIONS

GWENDOLYN BRYANT, MEMBERSHIP MANAGER

MEGHAN DUFFY NEWMAN, STEWARDSHIP MANAGER

CYNTHIA MERTON, DATABASE MANAGER

JODI SNYDER, CORPORATE PARTNERSHIP COORDINATOR

CRYSTAL CLARK, DEVELOPMENT COORDINATOR

LISA ERTL, DEVELOPMENT ASSISTANT FOR PROSPECTS

EMILY MILLER, DEVELOPMENT ASSISTANT FOR
RECORDS MANAGEMENT

YVONNE TOOT, DEVELOPMENT ASSISTANT
FOR MEMBERSHIP

EDUCATION

SANDRA D. YOUNG, DIRECTOR OF EDUCATION

FINANCE

FRANK PEDITTO, CHIEF FINANCIAL OFFICER

JAY D. PECK, CONTROLLER

MICHAEL DOOLITTLE, DIRECTOR OF
INFORMATION TECHNOLOGY

ROBERT LARMORE, SENIOR SYSTEMS ENGINEER

HAZEL LEE, SYSTEMS ENGINEER

ABENA PURNELL-PRIOR, STAFF ACCOUNTANT

RENEE DOMAN, STAFF ACCOUNTANT

TRACY DINH, PAYROLL/STAFF ACCOUNTANT

MARKETING

SANDRA HORROCKS, DIRECTOR OF MARKETING
AND COMMUNICATIONS

TIFFANY MADDEN, ASSISTANT DIRECTOR OF
MARKETING AND COMMUNICATIONS

MARGIE SMITH, DIRECTOR OF MEDIA RELATIONS

SALLY KUTYLA, MANAGER OF VOLUNTEER SERVICES

EVELYN TAYLOR, WEB MANAGER

MOLLY CLARK, MARKETING COORDINATOR

KEISHA HUTCHINS, PUBLIC RELATIONS ASSISTANT

REBECCA CLEMENT, GROUP SALES MANAGER

OPERATIONS

JOHN X. FERNANDEZ, JR., DIRECTOR OF
OPERATIONS AND EXECUTIVE PRODUCER

DAN DURO, SENIOR PRODUCTION MANAGER

GREG BUCH, PRODUCTION MANAGER

ALEX BAGNALL, ASSISTANT PRODUCTION MANAGER

DAVID THIELE, ASSISTANT PRODUCTION MANAGER

HARRIET WEIL, ASSISTANT PRODUCTION MANAGER

TOM WARNER, HOUSE MANAGER

HUGH WALSH, HOUSE MANAGER

JESSICA HAPPEL, ASSISTANT HOUSE MANAGER

MAUREEN LYNCH, ASSISTANT HOUSE MANAGER

RICHARD TOBIN, ASSISTANT HOUSE MANAGER

JACK NIXON, CHIEF ENGINEER

LILLY SCHWARTZ, BOOKING MANAGER

ERIC HAEKER, OPERATIONS ASSOCIATE

STEVEN BERGQUIST, RESTAURANT ASSOCIATES,
GENERAL MANAGER

DEBBIE GLUCK, EVENT MANAGER

LEAH ORIOLO, PROJECT ASSISTANT FOR
OPENING CELEBRATION

PUBLICATIONS

NANCY L. HEBBLE, DIRECTOR OF PUBLICATIONS

DAVID UPDIKE, PUBLICATIONS MANAGER

SAMUEL M. YOUNG, PRINT MANAGER

TICKET PHILADELPHIA

MATTHEW COOPER, DIRECTOR OF TICKETING SERVICES

DANIEL AHEARN, JR., BOX OFFICE MANAGER

PATRICK CURRAN, ASSISTANT TREASURER FOR BOX OFFICE

THADDEUS DYNAKOWSKI, ASSISTANT TREASURER FOR
BOX OFFICE

PATRICIA O'CONNOR, ASSISTANT TREASURER FOR
BOX OFFICE

CATHERINE PAPPAS, MANAGER OF SUBSCRIBER SERVICES

KEITH CONALLEN, ASSISTANT MANAGER OF
SUBSCRIBER SERVICES

MAUREEN KEARNEY, SUBSCRIBER SERVICES REPRESENTATIVE

ROBERT BOYD, SUBSCRIBER SERVICES REPRESENTATIVE

MIKE SMITH, SUBSCRIBER SERVICES REPRESENTATIVE

MICHELLE GUIM, SUBSCRIBER SERVICES REPRESENTATIVE

RICHARD PEEL, MANAGER OF TELEPHONE SERVICES

JAMES BRUNO, ASSISTANT MANAGER OF
TELEPHONE SERVICES

PATTY RODRIGUEZ, ADMINISTRATIVE ASSISTANT